Streamlines: Selected Readings on Single Topics

Mass Culture and Electronic Media

Streamlines: Selected Readings on Single Topics

Mass Culture and Electronic Media

Marjorie Ford
Stanford University

Jon Ford
College of Alameda

Houghton Mifflin Company

Boston   New York

SENIOR SPONSORING EDITOR: Suzanne Phelps Weir
SENIOR ASSOCIATE EDITOR: Janet Edmonds
EDITORIAL ASSISTANT: Tamara Jachimowicz
EDITORIAL PRODUCTION COORDINATOR: Carla Thompson
PRODUCTION/DESIGN COORDINATOR: Jennifer Meyer Dare
SENIOR MANUFACTURING COORDINATOR: Priscilla J. Abreu
SENIOR MARKETING MANAGER: Nancy Lyman

COVER DESIGN: Rebecca Fagan
COVER IMAGE: Jim Wehtje/PhotoDisc

Library of Congress Catalog Card Number: 98-72028
ISBN: 0-395-86803-3

23456789–CS–02 01 00 99

CONTENTS

A series of four books on intriguing, relevant topics, *Streamlines: Selected Readings on Single Topics* are an innovation among composition textbooks for college writing courses. Designed to encourage creativity, critical thinking, and research in writing classrooms, the series presents a range of texts to choose from: classic and contemporary essays, literature, journalistic writing, research-based writing, and student essays. The books can be used individually or in combination. Each book allows instructors to delve deeply into single topics— Learning, Health, the Natural World, and Mass Culture and Electronic Media—while allowing for a variety of teaching approaches. Some instructors may assign one or two of the books in addition to readings in a general purpose reader and a rhetoric/handbook to provide strong thematic focus for the course. Other instructors may feel comfortable setting aside three or four weeks toward the end of a semester to investigate a single issue, perhaps with a goal of a final project such as a longer oral or written assignment. Yet other instructors may structure their course around several of the books, perhaps making cross-references between related texts in different volumes of the series.

Format

Streamlines' major strengths include accessibility and ease of use, which stem in part from their consistent format. Each book is approximately 130 pages long, includes 13 to 16 readings, and contains a substantial, but not overwhelming, apparatus—a brief introduction, five study and discussion questions, and two suggestions for writing projects for each reading selection. Several topics for thought, research, and writing at the end of each book help students synthesize the individual selections. The books introduce students to the subject matter of the volume with an initial poem. Every book is divided into four sections, which contain several thematically related works.

The Individual Readers

Learning This volume contains readings that address fundamental questions that philosophers, educators, and psychologists ask about how and why people learn, and examine events and attitudes that can make learning difficult as well as pleasurable. The issue of learning (both in and out of the classroom) is especially relevant for first-year composition students to examine in depth. The first section of the reader, "Learning from Experience," explores the learning that results from the revelations that arise from learning experiences. "Learning at School," the next section, focuses on classrooms and explores different aspects of them. "Learning and Diversity" considers ways that language, cultural, and class differences become issues in education, while the final section, "Thinking About How We Learn," looks at how intelligence is defined and how effective education programs can help to build strong communities.

Health   Students are concerned about many health issues, and we have tried to confront some of these concerns in this volume. The selections engage interest by closely viewing health concerns that are foremost in students' minds. The first section, "Doctors," examines how both caring, supportive relations with physicians and self-awareness figure into recovery processes. "Self-Image and High-Risk Behavior" discusses relationships among self-esteem, body image, and wellness, while the third section, "Mental Health," examines relationships between psychological stress and physical illness as well as some of the symptoms, causes, and consequences of mental disorders such as depression and manic depression. The final section, "Healing and Community," provides a broader perspective on ways that doctors and patients can work together to create caring communities dedicated to good health.

The Natural World   Nature inspires people of all ages; it is also an area for controversies and concerns about the use and preservation of species and ecosystems. This volume begins with an exploration of "The Experience of Nature," which includes inspirational narratives of travels in nature. The second section, "Nature and the Scientific Mind," explores the ways scientists perceive nature and theorize about natural processes. "Environmental Issues: Protection and Preservation" presents students with controversies surrounding pollution, environmental disasters, and the movement to protect the earth and its species. Finally, in "Nature and the Philosophical Imagination," students are introduced to meditative essays that reflect on philosophical and spiritual meanings that can be found through contact with nature.

Mass Culture and Electronic Media   At the heart of many students' cultural experiences are the electronic media—particularly radio, television, CDs, and the Internet. We begin this volume with "Cult Heroes and Icons," which presents readings that bridge discussions of the older heroes of the mass media of cartoons and comic books with heroes of the newer media. The second section, "Family, Gender, and the Electronic Media," provides analysis of the impact of the electronic media on women and family life. "Ethnicity and Electronic Media" reflects on media images of minority groups. Finally, in "Reality Re-configured: Reading the New Electronic Media," media theorists and researchers discuss how television and the Internet influence our perceptions of reality and suggest ways to "read" the media insightfully in order to accurately discern underlying messages.

We would like to thank Alison Zetterquist and Janet Edmonds at Houghton Mifflin, and our student writers. For helping us refine our ideas, we would also like to thank our reviewers:

James K. Bell, College of San Mateo
Donald Blount, University of South Carolina—Aiken
Keith Coplin, Colby Community College
Jan Delasara, Metropolitan State College of Denver
Patrick Dolan, Arapahoe Community College
Frank Fennell, Loyola University
Judith Funston, State University of New York at Potsdam
Sara McLaughlin, Texas Tech University
Denish Martone, New York University
Lawrence E. Musgrove, University of Southern Indiana
Julie Nichols, Okaloosa-Walton Community College
Pearlie M. Peters, Rider University
Katherine Ploeger, Modesto Junior College, California State
    University, Stanislaus
John Reilly, Loyola Marymount University
Patricia Roberts, Rivier College
Kristen Snoddy, Indiana University, Kokomo
Jan Strever, Gonzaga University

M. F.
J. F.

It is television's dominant role in the family that anesthetizes the family into accepting its unhappy state.   **MARIE WINN**

Perhaps the visual quiescence of radio is related to the popularity of E-mail or electronic networking. Only the voice is made manifest, unmasking worlds that cannot—or dare not?—be seen.
                                                          PATRICIA WILLIAMS

What the epic poem did for ancient cultures, the romance for feudalism, and the novel for bourgeois society, the media—and especially television—now do for the commodified, bureaucratized world that is our present environment.   **ROBERT SCHOLES**

The electronic media permeate almost every facet of our lives. The average American spends three to four hours a day watching television and several more hours each week viewing films and videos, listening to music on CDs and radio, and using the Internet. It is not surprising that electronic media influence us in many ways, from the way people model their lifestyles on the characters they identify with in popular shows, to the increased rate of consumption of products heavily advertised on television, to the political opinions we hold. As consumers of mass media, we easily can become their victims through failing to consider how extensively our personality and values are being shaped by the media environment. Most people lack formal training in media analysis and response; only a tiny percentage of American youth are introduced to media criticism in primary or secondary school.

One of the goals of this anthology is to help you increase your understanding of electronic media and become media literate through becoming more conscious of the media and developing critical strategies for interpretation and evaluation. In this new age of computers, multimedia, and the Internet, citizens need to develop an understanding of how media communicate and pressure us in various ways. This understanding can free us to control the time we spend consuming media and to evaluate their content and influences more fully.

The essays in the four sections of this book reveal a variety of responses to the media and the myths created by media figures. Some of the writers are deeply critical of the impact that media have on our perceptions and values, and others are intrigued by the recent changes and future potential in electronic communications.

Cult Heroes and Icons

Similar to the way traditional religious devotees use icons (small symbolic paintings of religious figures and scenes) to create a physical and aesthetic focus for their meditations, many people today use the often-repeated situations and popular figures in mass culture to give concrete form to their beliefs and aspirations. This section presents essays that examine some of the enduring icons of American popular culture and attempt to define the sources of their popularity through a close analysis of their primary features and implied values. The first essay, novelist John Updike's "The Mystery of Mickey Mouse," explores the evolution of the simple, poignant style of Walt Disney's classic character, concluding that Mickey resonates strongly with the American people, embodying "America as it feels to itself— plucky, put-on, inventive, resilient, good-natured, game." Music critic Stanley Crouch presents a critical perspective on the music and career of Michael Jackson in the essay "The King of Narcissism." Crouch sees Jackson as a performer who lacks real talent, yet who is the producer of a powerful pop image and sound that has become progressively more disturbing, more suffused with the imagery and rhythms of totalitarianism. The final essay in this section, "The Age of the Female Icon," by columnist Holly Brubach, takes an upbeat view of the current popularity of the female icons whom many women perceive as role models: "If . . . our female icons seem to loom larger in our culture and to cast a longer shadow, perhaps it's because in so many cases their stories have had the urgency of history in the making."

Family, Gender, and the Electronic Media

The electronic media are often criticized for creating distorted representations of family life and gender issues. In a classic criticism of the influence of television, "Family Life," Marie Winn explains the process through which television reorganizes families, with parent-child interaction replaced by ritual interaction with favorite television shows and characters. Next, philosopher Sissela Bok examines the impact of the violence of television and films on children's ability to control their aggressive impulses.

Not all critics agree that television is responsible for the deterioration of the modern family and related social ills. Youth advocate Mike Males, in his recent essay "Who Us? Stop Blaming Kids and TV," takes the position that the real causes of youth misbehavior can be found in parental neglect and abuse.

Media analysts are just beginning to think critically about gender-based patterns of computer use and participation in on-line news groups and chat rooms. In her controversial essay "Men, Women, and Computers," Barbara Kantrowitz argues that the on-line world is both male-dominated and hostile to women. She believes that women can survive on-line only by grouping together in closed chat rooms or private news groups. Kantrowitz encourages both men and women to redefine their relationship to computers in a more "feminine" way and to use these machines primarily as creative instruments rather than as weapons for social and economic dominance.

Ethnicity and Electronic Media

Media analysts have made serious criticisms of the impact that television, radio, and popular music have had on ethnic minorities. Although the media feature some variety of ethnic heroes and icons, there still is much room for diversity. This section begins with a view of the past, as Henry Louis Gates, Jr., narrates personal experiences of growing up with television in the late 1950s. In his essay, "The Living Room," Gates describes how television brought his small-town family into the "ritual arena for the drama of race," presenting him with new images of whites and blacks and introducing him to the civil rights movement. In "Gangsta Culture," cultural critic bell hooks makes the point that the widespread criticism of the violent and misogynistic rap music produced by young black males ignores the fact that the works of these young recording artists are natural products of a patriarchal culture that supports values of violence, racism, and sexism as social norms.

Next, law professor Patricia J. Williams takes a critical look at right-wing, racially biased talk-format radio programming in her essay "Hate Radio." Williams concludes that rather than just providing a forum for people with an outdated perspective to exchange ideas, such programs, which she characterizes as "nostalgia crystallizing into a dangerous future," have increased the level of racial hatred in communities across the country, possibly triggering acts of violence against minorities. In this section's final essay, "Not in My Living Room," student writer Laura Chyu examines the role of Asian Americans in the electronic media, contrasting her experiences growing up as an Asian American with the observations of Henry Louis Gates, Jr., on African-American media images.

Reality Reconfigured: Reading the New Electronic Media

The essays in this section examine how the media change the way we think and perceive reality. Traditional skills and methods of decoding texts are based on the printed word; new skills and techniques need to be brought to bear to help us comprehend how the electronic media communicate and shape perceptions and thought. In "On Reading a Video Text," literary critic Robert Scholes presents some basic strategies and a case study of "reading" a television commercial, exploring the play of images and juxtapositions typical of this form in order to discover and interpret submerged values and mythical structure. Next, in "The Tales They Tell in Cyber-Space," reporter Jon Katz discusses both the texts that are emerging in the electronic medium of chat groups as well as the significance of this new form of publishing: "All over the world," he writes, "the gatekeepers are disintegrating as the few who always decided what stories the rest of us would hear are yielding to the millions telling their stories directly to one another." Taking a more critical perspective on the new media, Professors Byron Reeves and Clifford Nass, in their essay "Subliminal Images," point out how their research into the way that people relate to and learn from computers reveals that computers, because of the ability of software to interact with the user, have the potential to be even more manipulative and intrusive than television. They conclude that "ethical and legal issues abound" in relation to such manipulation. In the final essay, "Don't Look Back," software developer and electronic composer Steven Holtzman argues that despite the dangers and our fear of change, we shouldn't turn away from the new revelations and creative potential inherent in the new electronic media; rather, it is important that we "continue to explore these new digital worlds and seek to learn their true potential."

All Watched Over by
Machines of Loving Grace

RICHARD BRAUTIGAN

I like to think (and
the sooner the better!)
of a cybernetic meadow
where mammals and computers
live together in mutually   5
programming harmony
like pure water
touching clear sky

I like to think
(right now, please!)   10
of a cybernetic forest
filled with pines and electronics
where deer stroll peacefully
past computers
as if they were flowers   15
with spinning blossoms

I like to think
(it has to be!)
of a cybernetic ecology
where we are free of our labors   20
and joined back to nature,
returned to our mammal
brothers and sisters,
and all watched over
by machines of loving grace   25

Cult Heroes and Icons

The Mystery of Mickey Mouse

JOHN UPDIKE

Renowned as a novelist, essayist, and poet, John Updike (b. 1932) was born in Shillington, Pennsylvania, and completed his B.A. at Harvard. In 1959 he published his first novel, The Poorhouse Fair, *and he has been writing steadily ever since. Updike is best known for his sequence of novels about the career of Harry "Rabbit" Angstrom, high school athlete and suburbanite businessman:* Rabbit, Run *(1960),* Rabbit Redux *(1971),* Rabbit Is Rich *(1981), and* Rabbit at Rest *(1990). Although he writes about middle-class, suburban lives, Updike is a sophisticated stylist who continues to experiment with literary forms. His recent creations include a magic realist novel set in South America,* Brazil *(1994), and* Toward the End of Time *(1997), a science-fiction novel about an aging middle-class man who imagines a variety of alternate universes in which his life may be unfolding. In the following essay, Updike explores the evolving meaning of the familiar comic strip character, Mickey Mouse.*

It's all in the ears. When Mickey Mouse was born, in 1927, the world of early cartoon animation was filled with two-legged zoomorphic humanoids, whose strange half-black faces were distinguished one from another chiefly by the ears. Felix the Cat had pointed triangular ears and Oswald the Rabbit—Walt Disney's first successful cartoon creation, which he abandoned when his New York distributor, Charles Mintz, attempted to swindle him—had long floppy ears, with a few notches in the end to suggest fur. Disney's Oswald films, and the Alice animations that preceded them, had mice in them, with linear limbs, wiry tails, and ears that are oblong, not yet round. On the way back to California from New York by train, having left Oswald enmeshed for good in the machinations of Mr. Mintz, Walt and his wife Lillian invented another character based—the genesis legend claims—on the tame field mice that used to wander into Disney's old studio in Kansas City. His first thought was to call the mouse Mortimer; Lillian proposed instead the less pretentious name Mickey. Somewhere between Chicago and Los Angeles, the young couple concocted the plot of Mickey's first cartoon short, *Plane Crazy*, costarring Minnie and capitalizing on 1927's Lindbergh craze. The next short produced by Disney's fledgling studio—which included, besides himself and Lillian, his brother Roy and his old Kansas City associate Ub Iwerks—was *Gallopin' Gaucho*, and introduced a fat and wicked cat who did not yet wear the prosthesis that would give him his name of Pegleg Pete. The third short, *Steamboat Willie*, incorporated that brand-new novelty, a sound track, and was released first in 1928. Mickey Mouse entered

1

history, as the most persistent and pervasive figment of American popular culture in this century.

His ears are two solid black circles, no matter the angle at which he holds his head. Three-dimensional images of Mickey Mouse—toy, dolls, or the papier-mâché heads the grotesque Disneyland Mickeys wear—make us uneasy, since the ears inevitably exist edgewise as well as frontally. These ears properly belong not to three-dimensional space but to an ideal realm of notation, of symbolization, of cartoon resilience and indestructibility. In drawings, when Mickey is in profile, one ear is at the back of his head like a spherical ponytail, or like a secondary bubble in a computer-generated Mandelbrot set. We accept it, as we accepted Li'l Abner's hair always being parted on the side facing the viewer. A surreal optical consistency is part of the cartoon world, halfway between our world and the plane of pure signs, of alphabets and trademarks.

In the sixty-four years since Mickey Mouse's image was promulgated, the ears, though a bit more organically irregular and flexible than the classic 1930s appendages, have not been essentially modified. Many other modifications have, however, overtaken that first crude cartoon, born of an era of starker stylizations. White gloves, like the gloves worn in minstrel shows, appeared after those first, to cover the black hands. The infantile bare chest and shorts with two buttons were phased out in the forties. The eyes have undergone a number of changes, most drastically in the late thirties, when, some historians mistakenly claim, they acquired pupils. Not so: the old eyes, the black oblongs that acquired a nick of reflection in the sides, *were* the pupils; the eye whites filled the entire space beneath Mickey's cap of black, its widow's peak marking the division between these enormous oculi. This can be seen clearly in the face of the classic Minnie; when she bats her eyelids, their lashed shades cover over the full width of what might be thought to be her brow. But all the old animated animals were built this way from Felix the Cat on; Felix had lower lids, and the Mickey of *Plane Crazy* also. So it was an evolutionary misstep that, beginning in 1938, replaced the shiny black pupils with entire oval eyes, containing pupils of their own. No such mutation has overtaken Pluto, Goofy, or Donald Duck. The change brought Mickey closer to us humans, but also took away something of his vitality, his alertness, his bugeyed cartoon readiness for adventure. It made him less abstract, less iconic, more merely cute and dwarfish. The original Mickey, as he scuttles and bounces through those early animated shorts, was angular and wiry, with much of the impudence and desperation of a true rodent. He was gradually rounded to the proportions of a child, a regression sealed by his fifties manifestation as the genius of the children's television show *The Mickey Mouse Club*, with its live Mouseketeers. Most of the artists who depict Mickey today, though too young to have grown up, as I did, with his old form, have instinctively

2

3

reverted to it; it is the bare-chested basic Mickey, with his yellow shoes and oval buttons on his shorts, who is the icon, beside whom his modified later version is a mere mousy trousered pipsqueak.

His first, iconic manifestation had something of Chaplin to it; he 4 was the little guy, just over the border of the respectable. His circular ears, like two minimal cents, bespeak the smallest economic unit, the overlookable democratic man. His name has passed into the language as a byword for the small, the weak—a "Mickey Mouse operation" means an undercapitalized company or minor surgery. Children of my generation—wearing our Mickey Mouse watches, prying pennies from our Mickey Mouse piggy banks (I won one in a third-grade spelling bee, my first intellectual triumph), following his running combat with Pegleg Pete in the daily funnies, going to the local movie-house movies every Saturday afternoon and cheering when his smiling visage burst onto the screen to introduce a cartoon—felt Mickey was one of us, a bridge to the adult world of which Donald Duck was, for all of his childish sailor suit, an irascible, tyrannical member. Mickey didn't seek trouble, and he didn't complain; he rolled with the punches, and surprised himself as much as us when, as in *The Little Tailor,* he showed warrior resourcefulness and won, once again, a blushing kiss from dear, all but identical Minnie. His minimal, decent nature meant that he would yield, in the Disney animated cartoons, the starring role to combative, sputtering Donald Duck and even to Goofy, with his "gawshes" and Gary Cooper–like gawkiness. But for an occasional comeback like the "Sorcerer's Apprentice" episode of *Fantasia,* and last year's rather souped-up *The Prince and the Pauper,* Mickey was through as a star by 1940. But as with Marilyn Monroe when her career was over, his life as an icon gathered strength. The American that is not symbolized by that imperial Yankee Uncle Sam is symbolized by Mickey Mouse. He is America as it feels to itself—plucky, put-on, inventive, resilient, good-natured, game.

Like America, Mickey has a lot of black blood. This fact was revealed 5 to me in conversation by Saul Steinberg, who, in attempting to depict the racially mixed reality of New York streets for the supersensitive and raceblind *New Yorker* of the sixties and seventies, hit upon scribbling numerous Mickeys as a way of representing what was jauntily and scruffily and unignorably there. From just the way Mickey swings along in his classic, trademark pose, one three-fingered gloved hand held on high, he is jiving. Along with round black ears and yellow shoes, Mickey has soul. Looking back to such early animations as the early Looney Tunes' Bosko and Honey series (1930–36) and the Arab figures in Disney's own *Mickey in Arabia* of 1932, we see that blacks were drawn much like cartoon animals, with round button noses and great white eyes creating the double arch of the curious peaked skullcaps. Cartoon characters' rubberiness, their jazziness, their cheerful buoyance and idleness, all chimed with popular images of African

Americans, earlier embodied in minstrel shows and in Joel Chandler Harris's tales of Uncle Remus, which Disney was to make into an animated feature, *Song of the South,* in 1946.

Up to 1950, animated cartoons, like films in general, contained   6
caricatures of blacks that would be unacceptable now; in fact, *Song of the South* raised objections from the NAACP [National Association for the Advancement of Colored People] when it was released. In recent reissues of *Fantasia,* two Nubian centaurettes and a pickaninny centaurette who shines the others' hooves have been edited out. Not even the superb crows section of *Dumbo* would be made now. But there is a sense in which all animated cartoon characters are more or less black. Steven Spielberg's hectic tribute to animation, *Who Framed Roger Rabbit?,* has them all, from the singing trees of Silly Symphonies to Daffy Duck and Woody Woodpecker, living in a Los Angeles ghetto, Toonville. As blacks were second-class citizens with entertaining qualities, so the animated shorts were second-class movies, with unreal actors who mocked and illuminated from underneath the real world, the live-actor cinema. Of course, even in a ghetto there are class distinctions. Porky Pig and Bugs Bunny have homes that they tend and defend, whereas Mickey started out, like those other raffish stick figures and dancing blots from the twenties, as a free spirit, a wanderer. As Richard Schickel has pointed out, "The locales of his adventures throughout the 1930s ranged from the South Seas to the Alps to the deserts of Africa. He was, at various times, a gaucho, teamster, explorer, swimmer, cowboy, fireman, convict, pioneer, taxi driver, castaway, fisherman, cyclist, Arab, football player, inventor, jockey, storekeeper, camper, sailor, Gulliver, boxer," and so forth. He was, in short, a rootless vaudevillian who would play any part that the bosses at Disney Studios assigned him. And though the comic strip, which still persists, has fitted him with all of a white man's household comforts and headaches, it is as an unencumbered drifter whistling along on the road of hard knocks, ready for whatever adventure waits at the next turning, that he lives in our minds.

Cartoon characters have soul as Carl Jung defined it in his *Arche-*   7
types and the Collective Unconscious: "soul is a life-giving demon who plays his elfin game above and below human existence." Without the "leaping and twinkling of the soul," Jung says, "man would rot away in his greatest passion, idleness." The Mickey Mouse of the thirties shorts was a whirlwind of activity, with a host of unsuspected skills and a reluctant heroism that rose to every occasion. Like Chaplin and Douglas Fairbanks and Fred Astaire, he acted out our fantasies of endless nimbleness, of perfect weightlessness. Yet withal, there was nothing aggressive or self-promoting about him, as there was about Popeye. Disney, interviewed in the thirties, said, "Sometimes I've tried to figure out why Mickey appealed to the whole world. Everybody's tried to

figure it out. So far as I know, nobody has. He's a pretty nice fellow who never does anybody any harm, who gets into scrapes through no fault of his own, but always manages to come up grinning." This was perhaps Disney's image of himself: for twenty years he did Mickey's voice in the films, and would often say, "There's a lot of the Mouse in me." Mickey was a character created with his own pen, and nurtured on Disney's memories of his mouse-ridden Kansas City studio and of the Missouri farm where his struggling father tried for a time to make a living. Walt's humble, scrambling beginnings remained embodied in the mouse, whom the Nazis, in a fury against the Mickey-inspired Allied legions (the Allied code word on D-Day was "Mickey Mouse"), called "the most miserable ideal ever revealed . . . mice are dirty."

But was Disney, like Mickey, just "a pretty nice fellow"? He was   8
until crossed in his driving perfectionism, his Napoleonic capacity to marshal men and take risks in the service of an artistic and entrepreneurial vision. He was one of those great Americans, like Edison and Henry Ford, who invented themselves in terms of a new technology. The technology—in Disney's case, film animation—would have been there anyway, but only a few driven men seized the full possibilities and made empires. In the dozen years between *Steamboat Willie* and *Fantasia,* the Disney studios took the art of animation to heights of ambition and accomplishment it would never have reached otherwise, and Disney's personal zeal was the animating force. He created an empire of the mind, and its emperor was Mickey Mouse.

The thirties were Mickey's conquering decade. His image circled   9
the globe. In Africa, tribesmen painfully had tiny mosaic Mickey Mouses inset into their front teeth, and a South African tribe refused to buy soap unless the cakes were embossed with Mickey's image, and a revolt of some native bearers was quelled when the safari masters projected some Mickey Mouse cartoons for them. Nor were the high and mighty immune to Mickey's elemental appeal—King George V and Franklin Roosevelt insisted that all film showings they attended include a dose of Mickey Mouse. But other popular phantoms, like Felix the Cat, have faded, where Mickey has settled into the national collective consciousness. The television program revived him for my children's generation, and the theme parks make him live for my grandchildren's. Yet survival cannot be imposed through weight of publicity; Mickey's persistence springs from something unhyped, something timeless in the image that has allowed it to pass in status from a fad to an icon.

To take a bite out of our imaginations, an icon must be simple. The   10
ears, the wiggly tail, the red shorts, give us a Mickey. Donald Duck and Goofy, Bugs Bunny and Woody Woodpecker are inextricably bound up with the draftsmanship of the artists who make them move and squawk, but Mickey floats free. It was Claes Oldenburg's pop art that first alerted me to the fact the Mickey Mouse had passed out of the

realm of commercially generated image into that of artifact. A new
Disney gadget, advertised on television, is a camera-like box that
spouts bubbles when a key is turned; the key consists of three circles,
two mounted on a larger one, and the image is unmistakably Mickey.
Like yin and yang, like the Christian cross and the star of Israel,
Mickey can be seen everywhere—a sign, a rune, hieroglyphic trace of
a secret power, an electricity we want to plug into. Like totem poles,
like African masks, Mickey stands at that intersection of abstraction
and representation where magic connects.

   Usually cartoon figures do not age, and yet their audience does age,   11
as generation succeeds generation, so that a weight of allusion and
sentimental reference increases. To the movie audiences of the early
thirties, Mickey Mouse was a piping-voiced live wire, the latest thing
in entertainment; by the time of *Fantasia* he was already a sentimental figure, welcomed back. *The Mickey Mouse Club,* with its slightly
melancholy pack leader, Jimmie Dodd, created a Mickey more re-
moved and marginal than in his first incarnation. The generation that
watched it grew up into the rebels of the sixties, to whom Mickey became camp, a symbol of U.S. cultural fast food, with a touch of the old
rodent raffishness. Politically, Walt, stung by the studio strike of 1940,
moved to the right, but Mickey remains one of the thirties proletariat,
not uncomfortable in the cartoon-rickety, cheerfully verminous crash
pads of the counterculture. At the Florida and California theme parks,
Mickey manifests himself as a short real person wearing an awkward
giant head, costumed as a ringmaster; he is in danger, in these
nineties, of seeming not merely venerable kitsch but part of the great
trash problem, one more piece of visual litter being moved back and
forth by the bulldozers of consumerism.

   But never fear, his basic goodness will shine through. Beyond re-   12
call, perhaps, is the simple love felt by us of the generation that grew
up with him. He was five years my senior and felt like a playmate.
I remember crying when the local newspaper, cutting down its comic
pages to help us win World War II, eliminated the Mickey Mouse strip.
I was old enough, nine or ten, or write an angry letter to the editor. In
fact, the strips had been eliminated by the votes of a readership poll,
and my indignation and sorrow stemmed from my incredulous reali-
zation that not everybody loved Mickey Mouse as I did. In an account
of my boyhood written over thirty years ago, "The Dogwood Tree," I
find these sentences concerning another boy, a rival: "When we both
collected Big Little Books, he outbid me for my supreme find (in the
attic of a third boy), the first Mickey Mouse. I can still see that book. I
wanted it so badly, its paper tan with age and its drawings done in Disney's primitive style, when Mickey's black chest is naked like a child's
and his eyes are two nicked oblongs." And I once tried to write a short
story called "A Sensation of Mickey Mouse," trying to superimpose on
adult experience, as a shiver-inducing revenant, that indescribable

childhood sensation—a rubbery taste, a licorice smell, a feeling of supernatural clarity and close-in excitation that Mickey Mouse gave me, and gives me, much dimmed by the years, still. He is a "genius" in the primary dictionary sense of "an attendant spirit," with his vulnerable bare black chest, his touchingly big yellow shoes, the mysterious place at the back of his shorts where his tail came out, the little cleft cushion of a tongue, red as a valentine and glossy as candy, always peeping through the catenary curves of his undiscourageable smile. Not to mention his ears.

QUESTIONS FOR DISCUSSION

1   What does Updike mean by the "surreal optical consistency" of cartoons?

2   How does Updike trace the physical evolution of Mickey Mouse throughout the sixty-four years of his existence? How do modern artists portray him? In what ways has Mickey's meaning changed for the different generations that came of age during this period?

3   How does Updike compare Mickey to Charlie Chaplin, the "little guy" of early silent films?

4   In what sense does Mickey have "a lot of black blood"? Are Updike's arguments and examples convincing here?

5   How does the narrative of Updike's personal experiences with Mickey in the final paragraph help to define the true mystery of the mouse and his lasting appeal?

IDEAS FOR WRITING

1   Updike comments that Walt Disney created "an empire of the mind, and its emperor was Mickey Mouse." Write an essay in which you discuss the ways in which Disney's creations and marketing have influenced people around the world.

2   Write an analysis of this essay that focuses on Updike's writing style. How do his lengthy, carefully coordinated sentences, his use of figurative language, and his choice of words help him to make his points? What other aspects of his style did you find effective?

The King of Narcissism

STANLEY CROUCH

*Born in Los Angeles, Stanley Crouch (b. 1945) was interested in
jazz and drama as a young man; he dropped out of college to work
as an actor, writer, and jazz drummer. Although he was poet in
residence and an instructor of jazz history, literature, and drama at
the Claremont Colleges in California from 1969 to 1975, his primary
professional interests have been essay writing and reviewing. Crouch
began his career by publishing pieces in black nationalist periodicals
such as* Liberator *and* Black World, *but he soon became disillusioned
with political radicalism and racial separatism. Moving to New York
in 1975, he began writing music columns and book reviews for the*
Village Voice; *he has also written for the* New Yorker, Forbes, *and the*
New Republic. *Crouch has published a book on race relations,* The
All-American Skin Game, Or, the Decoy of Race *(1995), as well as a
collection of essays,* Notes of a Hanging Judge: Essays and Reviews,
1979–1989 *(1990). As the titles of his books suggest, Crouch can be a
rigorous and opinionated critic with strong views on issues related
to popular culture and the politics of race. The following essay is
included in Crouch's new collection,* Always in Pursuit *(1998). It was
first published in the* New Republic *under the title "Hooked: Michael
Jackson, Moby Dick of Pop" (1995). Here Crouch takes aim at the
famous recording star, making crucial distinctions between the
"big beat" quality of pop music and more traditional forms such as
blues and jazz.*

It used to be that if one didn't hurry up and say something about an
event, the op-ed scow was gone, leaving the slowpoke commentator
at the dock. But now, with the oceanic marketing campaigns calcu-
lated to continually flop up sales, one can put two cents in and be
right on time for months. It is an unexpected variation on Americans
of the nineteenth century mourning Abraham Lincoln for months
after his assassination because national communication was then
like molasses in January. Now the question is just how much time a
product can maintain a position at the top of the huckster's wave, how
much media space it can dominate, whether or not it has the strength
to rise and disappear, rise and disappear, like a marlin, pulling the
ship of public boredom on and on, exciting the crew until—Lord
have mercy on us!—it ends up on the deck, not really a real fish but a
motorized piece of counterfeit so many have been trained to admire
and drool over even so.

Michael Jackson almost seems meant to help us understand the
complications of our basic myths and our perennial shortcomings.
But because we Americans often miss the elements of sensibility that

connect us, accepting false fire walls of division, we find it hard to see beyond the decoys of race, class, religion, and genitalia. It is perilous to miss those transcending essences, be they good or bad. Those essences are at the nub of our perpetually embattled democratic grandeur and our equally persistent childishness. No one, regardless of the point of social origin, is automatically beyond either the pinnacles or the spiritual sink holes of these United States—least of all our media figures. That is where the most magnified entertainer in the world comes in, because Jackson represents both the hard facts of open opportunity and the swollen visions of self-worth that have evolved in our narcissistic culture. As a show business product, he embodies the American dream of rising from nowhere to great wealth and mass adulation, but Jackson's recent work also reveals how easily the self-pitying anger that underlies totalitarian paranoia can seep into the content of popular entertainment.

The King of Pop is a man who would spend a long time in jail if he were sentenced to counting his riches dollar by dollar. He is an entertainer whom we have watched rise from an itty-bitty cute kid to a man self-made—or remade—quite remarkably by modern surgical techniques, all the while maintaining his celebrated submarine position in the pop music quicksand of adolescent emotion. Jackson extended his stardom by adding to his concerts and repertoire all the basic trends of his idiom and the slogans that pass for ideas. Always a mediocre singer given to progressively unimaginative phrasing and overstatement, Jackson will deliver a shallow version of gospel and some maudlin rhythm and blues, use the harsh bravado of rock inflection, posture as a love child reciting the pieties necessary for world peace, stoop to the vulgar gestures that are a counterfeit shorthand for lower-class rage, and execute a few interesting dance steps that serve as interludes within a choreographed synthesis of cheerleading moves, navy signaling without flags, and aerobic exercise. His work is a summation of the inflated failure that now dominates our popular arts, where the value of youth is hysterically championed at the expense of a mature sense of life. This exploits the insecurities of young people by telling them, over and over, that never growing up is the best defense against an oppressive world in which fun isn't given its proper due.

While Jackson's millions allow him to have fantasy kingdoms built, he also usurps the mantle of wealthy nut that Howard Hughes once wore with such unflagging madness. Like Hughes, Jackson also suffers from the distinct kind of paranoia that those who must face legions of jealousy sometimes orchestrate into endless symphonies of plots and subplots, ranging from the press to the government. The alienation that comes with vast success builds upon the familiar theme of the poor little rich kid and becomes the basis for innumerable expressions of complaint focused on the beleaguered tycoon, the adult who sits atop a kingdom of cash angrily trying to duck those who would bloody and destroy him.

   This paranoia has not been missed, even in the world of rock crit-   5
icism, where posterior-licking and the exaggerations of aesthetic
value are assiduously taught in the boot camps of preparation for
media employment. Though there was some understandable alarm
expressed when Jackson's gargantuan poor-mouthing and his lyrics
were examined in the new double-album, *HIStory,* even noting the
fascist imagery of the promotional video, what all those rock critics
missed was the problem at the center of pop music, which is the
function of its incantational rhythms.

   Incantation always has two audience possibilities in our culture: 6
one is the collective fused into a throbbing vitality through the repeat-
ing groove of a syncopated dance-beat; the other is the transformation
of individuals into a mindless mass of putty in the hands of a band or
a central figure. The distinction is very important because the vital collective is the highest achievement of dance-oriented rhythm. Essential
to that vitality is the expression of adult emotion. While blues might
also have simple musical elements similar to those pop has derived
from it, blues is fundamentally a music that fights self-pity and even
holds it up to ridicule, the singer scorning all self-deceptive attempts
at ducking responsibility for at least part of the bad state of affairs.

   In jazz, for another example, the rhythmic phenomenon of swing is   7
posed as an antidote to the sentimentality of the popular song, with
the improvisation allowing for collective inventions that insert emotional irony and complexity into the music. The evolution of pop
music is quite different because, far more often than not, the rhythm
is used to reinforce the sentimentality of the material. Those pop
rhythms now arrive in a form that has largely submitted to the
mechanical, often using electronic, programmed "drums" for static
pulsations that never interact with the rest of the music, a supreme
example of the very alienation it so successfully foments.

   It is because of the subordination of everything to the beat that the   8
lyrics so often go by barely noticed. When they are noticed, especially
when expressing the choked-up, immature resentment of a demand-
ing adult world in which problems are protean, the words either become anthems of estrangement or bludgeons against some vision of
corrupt and hypocritical authority. But, as with fascism, the authority
of a mass "conspiracy"—of bankers, lawyers, politicians, educators,
law enforcement, and so on—is rejected through obeisance to a figure
of gargantuan certitude. That is where the big beat of pop and the big
idol of the rock star meet in the fascist garden of dance-oriented
totalitarianism. Michael Jackson has been evolving in this direction
over the last few years, one video after another showing either the
world or his opposition melting into mass chorus lines overwhelmed
by his magical leadership. We see this most clearly in the promotional
video for *HIStory,* where Jackson marches in front of legions of troops,
children scream that they love him, and a huge statue of the King of
Pop, one as ugly as any Hitler, Stalin, or Mao would have appreciated,

is unveiled. We understand in clear terms the assertion that Hitler was the first rock star because of the way his rallies used technology to create hypnotic rituals of enormously magnified passion.

The Indian poet and philosopher Tagore once observed that the invention of the penknife leaped past the centuries of evolution that resulted in the claw, but that we often find ourselves in a world where those with the penknife mentalities of adolescents command weapons of destruction that they aren't mature enough to handle. When we make those who remain easily embittered little boys into idols by genuflecting before a charisma that has negligible adult application, we shouldn't be surprised at the point of their deciding that they should lead the world into a resurrection of an Eden through which they will walk in the cool of the day, omnipotent as the jealous God of the Old Testament.

QUESTIONS FOR DISCUSSION

1 Explain the extended nautical metaphor in the first paragraph. In light of the rest of the essay, what do the images of wave, marlin, ship, and crew signify?

2 In his third paragraph, Crouch attempts to define the kind of exploitation of adolescent emotion that made Jackson "the King of Pop." Do you agree that what he describes is a form of exploitation?

3 Crouch provides a very brief history of Jackson's career. How do the facts of Jackson's career help to explain the entertainer's broad appeal as well as his paranoia?

4 How and why does Crouch compare Michael Jackson to both the eccentric financier Howard Hughes and totalitarian leaders such as Hitler and Mao? Does either of these comparisons seem justified?

5 How does Crouch contrast the use of "incantational rhythms" or beat and the response to sentimentality in blues and jazz to the "totalitarian" rhythm and sentiment in pop music?

IDEAS FOR WRITING

1 Read some reviews of Jackson's records and videos, and interview some of his fans. Then write a response to Crouch in which you either agree or disagree with him about the sources of Michael Jackson's popularity.

2 Crouch makes a general criticism of today's pop music idols through his comments about the "fascist garden of dance-oriented totalitarianism." Write an essay in which you argue for or against this view of the pop hero as a totalitarian and omnipotent cult leader.

The Age of the Female Icon

HOLLY BRUBACH

Holly Brubach (b. 1953) studied to become a dancer. After leaving her native Pittsburgh, she moved to New York City to dance professionally with experimental choreographers there. In New York she has worked as a choreographer, advertising copywriter, and television script writer. After an injury forced her early retirement from dance, Brubach began writing reviews about dance as well as essays on the popular arts, fashion, and travel. Her work has appeared in Mademoiselle, *the* Saturday Review, *the* New York Times Book Review, *and the* New York Times Magazine, *where she currently writes a weekly column. The following essay was published in a special issue of the* New York Times Magazine *in 1996 that focused on heroine worship.*

It's the 90's, and the pantheon we've built to house the women in our   1
minds is getting crowded. Elizabeth Taylor, Eleanor Roosevelt, Oprah Winfrey, Alanis Morissette, Indira Gandhi, Claudia Schiffer, Coco Chanel, Doris Day, Aretha Franklin, Jackie Onassis, Rosa Parks—they're all there, the dead and the living side by side, contemporaneous in our imaginations. On television and in the movies, in advertising and magazines, their images are scattered across the landscape of our everyday lives. Their presence is sometimes decorative, sometimes uplifting, occasionally infuriating. The criteria for appointment to this ad hoc hall of fame that takes up so much space in our thoughts and in our culture may at first glance appear to be utterly random. In fact, irrespective of their achievements, most of these women have been apotheosized primarily on the basis of their ability to appeal to our fantasies.

An icon is a human sound bite, and individual reduced to a name,   2
a face and an idea: Dale Evans, the compassionate cowgirl. In some cases, just the name and an idea suffice. Few people would recognize Helen Keller in a photograph, but her name has become synonymous with being blind and deaf to such an extent that she has inspired an entire category of jokes. Greta Garbo has gone down in the collective memory as an exalted enigma with a slogan about being alone. Asking a man if that's a gun in his pocket is all it takes to invoke Mae West. Catherine Deneuve's face, pictured on a stamp, is the emblem of France. Virginia Woolf has her own T-shirt. Naomi Campbell has her own doll. Celebrity being the engine that drives our culture, these women have been taken up by the media and made famous, packaged as commodities and marketed to a public eager for novelty and easily bored.

Many worthy women are acknowledged for their accomplishments   3
but never take on the status of an icon. . . . The sheer number of icons
now in circulation makes any attempt to catalogue them all impossible. . . . Our icons are by no means exclusively female, but the male
ones are perhaps less ubiquitous and more accessible. The pedestals
we put them on are lower; the service they are called on to perform is
somewhat different.

Like women, men presumably look to icons for tips that they can   4
take away and apply to their lives. The men who are elevated to the
status of icons are the ones who are eminently cool, whose moves the
average guy can steal. They do not prompt a fit of introspection
(much less of self-recrimination), as female icons often do in women.
What a male icon inspires in other men is not so much the desire to
be him as the desire to be accepted by him—to be buddies, to shoot
pool together, to go drinking. I have all this on good authority from a
man of my acquaintance who insists that, though regular guys may
envy, say, Robert Redford for his ability to knock women dead, what
they're thinking as they watch him in a movie is not "Hey, I wonder if
I have what it takes to do that, too," but "I wonder if Redford would
like to hang out with me."

Whereas women may look at an icon like Raquel Welch, whose ap-   5
peal is clearly to the male half of humanity, and ask themselves, "If
that's what's required to appeal to a man, have I got it, or can I get it?"
(The thought of hanging out with Welch—going shopping together or
talking about boyfriends—would, I think it's safe to say, never cross
most women's minds.)

An entire industry, called fashion, has grown up around the busi-   6
ness of convincing women that they need to remake themselves in
someone else's image: makeup and clothes and other products are
presented not as alterations but as improvements. The notion of appearance and personality as a project to be undertaken is inculcated
early on. A man may choose to ignore certain male icons; a woman has
no such luxury where the great majority of female icons are concerned. She must come to terms with them, defining herself in relation
to them—emulating some, rejecting others. In certain cases, a single
icon may exist for her as both an example and a reproach.

Our male icons are simply the latest entries in a tradition of long   7
standing, broad enough in any given era to encompass any number of
prominent men. But the current array of female icons is a recent phenomenon, the outgrowth of aspirations many of which date back no
more than 100 years.

What were the images of women that informed the life of a girl   8
growing up 200 years ago? It's hard for us to imagine the world before
it was wallpapered with ads, before it was inundated with all the
visual "information" that comes our way in the course of an average

day and competes with real people and events for our attention. There were no magazines, no photographs. In church, a girl would have seen renderings of the Virgin Mary and the saints. She may have encountered portraits of royalty, whose station, unless she'd been born an aristocrat, must have seemed even more unattainable than that of the saints. There were picturesque genre paintings depicting peasants and chambermaids, to be seen at the public salons, if any-one thought to bring a girl to them. But the most ambitious artists concentrated on pagan goddesses and mythological women, who, being Olympian, inhabited a plane so lofty that they were presumably immune to quotidian concerns. History and fiction, for the girl who had access to them, contained tales of women whose lives had been somewhat more enterprising and action-packed than those of the women she saw around her, but her knowledge of most women's ex-ploits in her own time would have been limited to hearsay: a woman had written a novel, a woman had played hostess to one of the great-est philosophers of the age and discussed ideas with him, a woman had disguised herself as a man and gone to war. Most likely, a girl would have modeled herself on a female relative, or on a woman in her community. The great beauty who set the standard by which others were measured would have been the one in their midst—the prettiest girl in town, whose fame was local.

Nineteenth-century icons like Sarah Bernhardt and George Sand   9
would have imparted no more in the way of inspiration; their careers were predicated on their talents, which had been bestowed by God. It was Florence Nightingale who finally provided an example that was practicable, one to which well-born girls could aspire, and hundreds of women followed her into nursing.

Today, the images of women confronting a girl growing up in our   10
culture are far more diverse, though not all of them can be interpreted as signs of progress. A woman who in former times might have served as the model for some painter's rendering of one or another pagan goddess is now deployed to sell us cars and soap. The great beauty has been chosen from an international field of contenders. At the movies, we see the stories of fictional women brought to life by real actresses whose own lives have become the stuff of fiction. In the news, we read about women running countries, directing corporations, and ventur-ing into outer space.

The conditions that in our century have made possible this prolif-   11
eration of female icons were of course brought on by the convergence of advances in women's rights and the growth of the media into an industry. As women accomplished the unprecedented, the press took them up and made them famous, trafficking in their accomplish-ments, their opinions, their fates. If, compared with the male icons of our time, our female icons seem to loom larger in our culture and

to cast a longer shadow, perhaps it's because in so many cases their stories have had the urgency of history in the making.

When it comes to looking at women, we're all voyeurs, men and women alike. Does our urge to study the contours of their flesh and the changes in their faces stem from some primal longing to be reunited with the body that gave us life? Women have been the immemorial repository of male fantasies—a lonesome role that many are nonetheless loath to relinquish, given the power it confers and the oblique satisfaction it brings. The curiosity and desire inherent in the so-called male gaze, deplored for the way it has objectified women in art and in films, are matched on women's part by the need to assess our own potential to be found beautiful and by the pleasure in putting ourselves in the position of the woman being admired.

Our contemporary images of women are descended from a centuries-old tradition and, inevitably, they are seen in its light. Women have often been universalized, made allegorical. The figure who represents Liberty, or Justice, to say nothing of Lust or Wrath, is a woman, not a man—a tradition that persists: there is no Mr. America. The unidentified woman in innumerable paintings—landscapes, genre scenes, mythological scenes—transcends her circumstances and becomes Woman. It's the particular that is customarily celebrated in men, and the general in woman. Even our collective notions of beauty reflect this: a man's idiosyncrasies enhance his looks; a woman's detract from hers.

"I'm every woman, it's all in me," Chaka Khan sings, and the chords in the bass modulate optimistically upward, in a surge of possibility. Not all that long ago, the notion that any woman could be every woman would have been dismissed as blatantly absurd, but to our minds it makes evident sense, in keeping with the logic that we can be anything we want to be—the cardinal rule of the human-potential movement and an assumption that in America today is so widely accepted and dearly held that it might as well be written into the Constitution. Our icons are at this point sufficiently plentiful that to model ourselves on only one of them would seem arbitrary and limiting, when in fact we can take charge in the manner of Katharine Hepburn, strut in the way we learned by watching Tina Turner, flirt in the tradition of Rita Hayworth, grow old with dignity in the style of Georgia O'Keeffe. In the spirit of post-modernism, we piece ourselves together, assembling the examples of several women in a single personality—a process that makes for some unprecedented combinations, like Madonna: the siren who lifts weights and becomes a mother. We contemplate the women who have been singled out in our culture and the permutations of femininity they represent. About to move on to the next century, we call on various aspects of them as we reconfigure our lives, deciding which aspects of our selves we want to take with us and which aspects we want to leave behind.

QUESTIONS FOR DISCUSSION

1   What social and psychological factors cause certain women to become icons of popular culture? Can you think of other causes?

2   How does Brubach define the term *icon,* and what examples does she give to clarify her definition? Can you think of other examples or qualities of the icon?

3   How does Brubach contrast today's cultural icons for women (and the ways that women relate to them) with male cultural icons? Do you think the contrast she makes is valid?

4   How does Brubach contrast the female icons available to women today to those available two hundred years ago? Does the change she describes seem altogether desirable to you? Why or why not?

5   How does Brubach use a cliché of the human-potential movement, "We can be anything we want to be," to clarify the new way that women perceive themselves through relating to a variety of available iconic figures? Are the examples she uses to clarify her point effective?

IDEAS FOR WRITING

1   Write an essay about a media or cultural iconic figure whom you admire or with whom you identify. Give examples of how the "icon" has influenced you to pattern your appearance, values, and lifestyle.

2   Write a response to Brubach in which you examine the desirability of identifying with and taking on qualities of iconic figures.

Family, Gender, and the Electronic Media

Family Life

MARIE WINN

*Marie Winn (b. 1936) was born in Prague, Czechoslovakia, and
came to the United States at the age of three. Educated at Columbia
University, Winn has worked primarily as a freelance writer specializ-
ing in the area of child development. Her articles have appeared in*
Parade, *the* New York Times Book Review, *and the* New York Times
Magazine. *Her books include children's stories and collections of songs
and play-centered activities; her major nonfiction works are* Children
Without Childhood *(1983),* The Plug-in Drug: Television, Children
and the Family *(1977, revised 1985), and* Unplugging the Plug-in
Drug *(1987). The following essay from* The Plug-in Drug *addresses
television's responsibility for the destruction of some of the vital
experiences of childhood: childhood games and family rituals.*

Less than forty years after the introduction of television into Amer-   1
ican society, a period that has seen the medium become so deeply in-
grained in American life that in at least one state the television set has
attained the rank of a legal necessity, safe from repossession in case of
debt along with clothes, cooking utensils, and the like, television
viewing has become an inevitable and ordinary part of daily life. Only
in the early years of television did writers and commentators have
sufficient perspective to separate the activity of watching television
from the actual content it offers the viewer. In those early days writers
frequently discussed the effects of television on family life. However,
a curious myopia afflicted those early observers: almost without exception they regarded television as a favorable, beneficial, indeed,
wondrous influence upon the family.

"Television is going to be a real asset in every home where there are   2
children," predicts a writer in 1949.

"Television will take over your way of living and change your chil-   3
dren's habits, but this change can be a wonderful improvement,"
claims another commentator.

"No survey's needed, of course, to establish that television has   4
brought the family together in one room," writes *The New York Times'*
television critic in 1949.

Each of the early articles about television is invariably accompa-   5
nied by a photograph or illustration showing a family cozily sitting
together before the television set, Sis on Mom's lap, Buddy perched on
the arm of Dad's chair, Dad with his arm around Mom's shoulder. Who
could have guessed that twenty or so years later Mom would be
watching a drama in the kitchen, the kids would be looking at cartoons in their room, while Dad would be taking in the ball game in the
living room?

Of course television sets were enormously expensive in those early   6
days. The idea that by 1982 more than half of all American families
would own two or more sets seemed preposterous. The splintering of
the multiple-set family was something the early writers could not
foresee. Nor did anyone imagine the number of hours children would
eventually devote to television, the changes television would effect
upon child-rearing methods, the increasing domination of family
schedules by children's viewing requirements—in short, the *power* of
television to dominate family life.

After the first years, as children's consumption of the new medium   7
increased, together with parental concern about the possible effects
of so much television viewing, a steady refrain helped to soothe and
reassure anxious parents. "Television always enters a pattern of influences that already exist: the home, the peer group, the school, the
church and culture generally," wrote the authors of an early and influential study of television's effects on children. In other words, if the
child's home life is all right, parents need not worry about the effects
of all that television watching.

But television did not merely influence the child; it deeply influ-   8
enced that "pattern of influences" everyone hoped would ameliorate
the new medium's effects. Home and family life have changed in
important ways since the advent of television. The peer group has
become television-oriented, and much of the time children spend
together is occupied by television viewing. Culture generally has been
transformed by television. Therefore it is improper to assign to television the subsidiary role its many apologists (too often members of the
television industry) insist it plays. Television is not merely one of a
number of important influences upon today's child. Through the
changes it has made in family life, television emerges as *the* important
influence in children's lives today.

The Quality of Family Life

Television's contribution to family life has been an equivocal one.   9
For while it has, indeed, kept the members of the family from dis-
persing, it has not served to bring them *together.* By its domination of
the time families spend together, it destroys the special quality that
distinguishes one family from another, a quality that depends to a
great extent on what a family *does,* what special rituals, games, recurrent jokes, familiar songs, and shared activities it accumulates.

"Like the sorcerer of old," writes Urie Bronfenbrenner, "the tele-   10
vision set casts its magic spell, freezing speech and action, turning the
living into silent statues so long as the enchantment lasts. The primary danger of the television screen lies not so much in the behavior
it produces—although there is danger there—as in the behavior it
prevents: the talks, the games, the family festivities and arguments

through which much of the child's learning takes place and through which his character is formed. Turning on the television set can turn off the process that transforms children into people."

Yet parents have accepted a television-dominated family life so   11
completely that they cannot see how the medium is involved in whatever problems they might be having. A first-grade teacher reports:

"I have one child in the group who's an only child. I wanted to find   12
out more about her family life because this little girl was quite isolated from the group, didn't make friends, so I talked to her mother. Well, they don't have time to do anything in the evening, the mother said. The parents come home after picking up the child at the baby-sitter's. Then the mother fixes dinner while the child watches TV. Then they have dinner and the child goes to bed. I said to this mother, 'Well, couldn't she help you fix dinner? That would be a nice time for the two of you to talk,' and the mother said, 'Oh, but I'd hate to have her miss "Zoom." It's such a good program!'"

Even when families make efforts to control television, too often its   13
very presence counterbalances the positive features of family life. A writer and mother of two boys aged 3 and 7 described her family's television schedule in an article in *The New York Times*:

> We were in the midst of a full-scale War. Every day was a new battle and every program was a major skirmish. We agreed it was a bad scene all around and were ready to enter diplomatic negotiations. . . . In principle we have agreed on 2½ hours of TV a day, "Sesame Street," "Electric Company" (with dinner gobbled up in between) and two half-hour shows between 7 and 8:30 which enables the grown-ups to eat in peace and prevents the two boys from destroying one another. Their pre-bedtime choice is dreadful, because, as Josh recently admitted, "There's nothing much on I really like." So . . . it's "What's My Line" or "To Tell the Truth." . . . Clearly there is a need for first-rate children's shows at this time. . . .

Consider the "family life" described here: Presumably the father   14
comes home from work during the "Sesame Street"–"Electric Company" stint. The children are either watching television, gobbling their dinner, or both. While the parents eat their dinner in peaceful privacy, the children watch another hour of television. Then there is only a half-hour left before bedtime, just enough time for baths, getting pajamas on, brushing teeth, and so on. The children's evening is regimented with an almost military precision. They watch their favorite programs, and when there is "nothing much on I really like," they watch whatever else is on—because *watching* is the important thing. Their mother does not see anything amiss with watching programs just for the sake of watching; she only wishes there were some first-rate children's shows on at those times.

Without conjuring up memories of the Victorian era with family   15
games and long, leisurely meals, and large families, the question

arises: isn't there a better family life available than this dismal, mechanized arrangement of children watching television for however long is allowed them, evening after evening?

Of course, families today still do *special* things together at times: go   16
camping in the summer, go to the zoo on a nice Sunday, take various trips and expeditions. But their *ordinary* daily life together is diminished—that sitting around at the dinner table, that spontaneous taking up of an activity, those little games invented by children on the spur of the moment when there is nothing else to do, the scribbling, the chatting, and even the quarreling, all the things that form the fabric of a family, that define a childhood. Instead, the children have their regular schedule of television programs and bedtime, and the parents have their peaceful dinner together.

The author of the article in the *Times* notes that "keeping a family   17
sane means mediating between the needs of both children and adults." But surely the needs of the adults are being better met than the needs of the children, who are effectively shunted away and rendered untroublesome, while their parents enjoy a life as undemanding as that of any childless couple. In reality, it is those very demands that young children make upon a family that lead to growth, and it is the way parents accede to those demands that builds the relationships upon which the future of the family depends. If the family does not accumulate its backlog of shared experiences, shared *everyday* experiences that occur and recur and change and develop, then it is not likely to survive as anything other than a caretaking institution.

Family Rituals

Ritual is defined by sociologists as "that part of family life that the   18
family likes about itself, is proud of and wants formally to continue." Another text notes that "the development of a ritual by a family is an index of the common interest of its members in the family as a group."

What has happened to family rituals, those regular, dependable,   19
recurrent happenings that gave members of a family a feeling of *belonging* to a home rather than living in it merely for the sake of convenience, those experiences that act as the adhesive of family unity far more than any material advantages?

Mealtime rituals, going-to-bed rituals, illness rituals, holiday rituals—   20
how many of these have survived the inroads of the television set?

A young woman who grew up near Chicago reminisces about her   21
childhood and gives an idea of the effects of television upon family rituals:

"As a child I had millions of relatives around—my parents both   22
come from relatively large families. My father had nine brothers and sisters. And so every holiday there was this great swoop-down of aunts,

uncles, and millions of cousins. I just remember how wonderful it used to be. These thousands of cousins would come and everyone would play and ultimately, after dinner, all the women would be in the front of the house, drinking coffee and talking, all the men would be in the back of the house, drinking and smoking, and all the kids would be all over the place, playing hide and seek. Christmas time was particularly nice because everyone always brought all their toys and games. Our house had a couple of rooms with go-through closets, so there were always kids running in a great circle route. I remember it was just wonderful.

"And then all of a sudden one year I remember becoming suddenly   23
aware of how different everything had become. The kids were no longer playing Monopoly or Clue or the other games we used to play together. It was because we had a television set which had been turned on for a football game. All of that socializing that had gone on previously had ended. Now everyone was sitting in front of the television set, on a holiday, at a family party! I remember being stunned by how awful that was. Somehow the television had become more attractive."

As families have come to spend more and more of their time   24
together engaged in the single activity of television watching, those rituals and pastimes that once gave family life its special quality have become more and more uncommon. Not since prehistoric times, when cave families hunted, gathered, ate, and slept, with little time remaining to accumulate a culture of any significance, have families been reduced to such a sameness.

Real People

It is not only the activities that a family might engage in together   25
that are diminished by the powerful presence of television in the home. The relationships of the family members to each other are also affected, in both obvious and subtle ways. The hours that children spend in a one-way relationship with television people, an involvement that allows for no communication or interaction, surely affect their relationships with real-life people.

Studies show the importance of eye-to-eye contact, for instance, in   26
real-life relationships, and indicate that the nature of one's eye-contact patterns, whether one looks another squarely in the eye or looks to the side or shifts one's gaze from side to side, may play a significant role in one's success or failure in human relationships. But no eye contact is possible in the child-television relationship, although in certain children's programs people purport to speak directly to the child and the camera fosters this illusion by focusing directly upon the person being filmed. (Mister Rogers is an example, telling the child, "I like you, you're special," etc.) How might such a distortion of

real-life relationships affect a child's development of trust, of openness, of an ability to relate well to other *real* people?

Bruno Bettelheim writes: 27

> Children who have been taught, or conditioned, to listen passively most of the day to the warm verbal communications coming from the TV screen, to the deep emotional appeal of the so-called TV personality, are often unable to respond to real persons because they arouse so much less feeling than the skilled actor. Worse, they lose the ability to learn from reality because life experiences are much more complicated than the ones they see on the screen. . . .

A teacher makes a similar observation about her personal viewing   28
experiences:

"I have trouble mobilizing myself and dealing with real people after   29
watching a few hours of television. It's just hard to make that transition from watching television to a real relationship. I suppose it's because there was no effort necessary while I was watching, and dealing with real people always requires a bit of effort. Imagine, then, how much harder it might be to do the same thing for a small child, particularly one who watches a lot of television every day."

But more obviously damaging to family relationships is the elimi-   30
nation of opportunities to talk, and perhaps more important, to argue, to air grievances, between parents and children and brothers and sisters. Families frequently use television to avoid confronting their problems, problems that will not go away if they are ignored but will only fester and become less easily resolvable as time goes on.

A mother reports: 31

"I find myself, with three children, wanting to turn on the TV set   32
when they're fighting. I really have to struggle not to do it because I feel that's telling them this is the solution to the quarrel—but it's so tempting that I often do it."

A family therapist discusses the use of television as an avoidance   33
mechanism:

"In a family I know the father comes home from work and turns on   34
the television set. The children come and watch with him and the wife serves them their meal in front of the set. He then goes and takes a shower, or works on the car or something. She then goes and has her own dinner in front of the television set. It's a symptom of a deeper-rooted problem, sure. But it would help them all to get rid of the set. It would be far easier to work on what the symptom really means without the television. The television simply encourages a double avoidance of each other. They'd find out more quickly what was going on if they weren't able to hide behind the TV. Things wouldn't necessarily be better, of course, but they wouldn't be anesthetized."

The decreased opportunities for simple conversation between par-   35
ents and children in the television-centered home may help explain

an observation made by an emergency room nurse at a Boston hospital. She reports that parents just seem to sit there these days when they come in with a sick or seriously injured child, although talking to the child would distract and comfort him. "They don't seem to know *how* to talk to their own children at any length," the nurse observes. Similarly, a television critic writes in *The New York Times*: "I had just a day ago taken my son to the emergency ward of a hospital for stitches above his left eye, and the occasion seemed no more real to me than Maalot or 54th Street, south-central Los Angeles. There was distance and numbness and an inability to turn off the total institution. I didn't behave at all; I just watched. . . ."

A number of research studies substantiate the assumption that   36
television interferes with family activities and the formation of family relationships. One survey shows that 78 percent of the respondents indicate no conversation taking place during viewing except at specified times such as commercials. The study notes: "The television atmosphere in most households is one of quiet absorption on the part of family members who are present. The nature of the family social life during a program could be described as 'parallel' rather than interactive, and the set does seem to dominate family life when it is on." Thirty-six percent of the respondents in another study indicated that television viewing was the only family activity participated in during the week.

In a summary of research findings on television's effect on family   37
interactions James Garbarino states: "The early findings suggest that television had a disruptive effect upon interaction and thus presumably human development. . . . It is not unreasonable to ask: 'Is the fact that the average American family during the 1950's came to include two parents, two children and a television set somehow related to the psychosocial characteristics of the young adults of the 1970's?'"

Undermining the Family

In its effect on family relationships, in its facilitation of parental with-   38
drawal from an active role in the socialization of their children, and in its replacement of family rituals and special events, television has played an important role in the disintegration of the American family. But of course it has not been the only contributing factor, perhaps not even the most important one. The steadily rising divorce rate, the increase in the number of working mothers, the decline of the extended family, the breakdown of neighborhoods and communities, the growing isolation of the nuclear family—all have seriously affected the family.

As Urie Bronfenbrenner suggests, the sources of family breakdown   39
do not come from the family itself, but from the circumstances in

which the family finds itself and the way of life imposed upon it by those circumstances. "When those circumstances and the way of life they generate undermine relationships of trust and emotional security between family members, when they make it difficult for parents to care for, educate and enjoy their children, when there is no support or recognition from the outside world for one's role as a parent and when time spent with one's family means frustration of career, personal fulfillment and peace of mind, then the development of the child is adversely affected," he writes.

But while the roots of alienation go deep into the fabric of American social history, television's presence in the home fertilizes them, encourages their wild and unchecked growth. Perhaps it is true that America's commitment to the television experience masks a spiritual vacuum, an empty and barren way of life, a desert of materialism. But it is television's dominant role in the family that anesthetizes the family into accepting its unhappy state and prevents it from struggling to better its condition, to improve its relationships, and to regain some of the richness it once possessed.   40

Others have noted the role of mass media in perpetuating an unsatisfactory *status quo*. Leisure-time activity, writes Irving Howe, "must provide relief from work monotony without making the return to work too unbearable; it must provide amusement without insight and pleasure without disturbance—as distinct from art which gives pleasure through disturbance. Mass culture is thus oriented towards a central aspect of industrial society: the depersonalization of the individual." Similarly, Jacques Ellul rejects the idea that television is a legitimate means of educating the citizen: "Education . . . takes place only incidentally. The clouding of his consciousness is paramount. . . ."   41

And so the American family muddles on, dimly aware that something is amiss but distracted from an understanding of its plight by an endless stream of television images. As family ties grow weaker and vaguer, as children's lives become more separate from their parents', as parents' educational role in their children's lives is taken over by television and schools, family life becomes increasingly more unsatisfying for both parents and children. All that seems to be left is love, an abstraction that family members *know* is necessary but find great difficulty giving each other because the traditional opportunities for expressing love within the family have been reduced or destroyed.   42

For contemporary parents, love toward each other has increasingly come to mean successful sexual relations, as witnessed by the proliferation of sex manuals and sex therapists. The opportunities for manifesting other forms of love through mutual support, understanding, nurturing, even, to use an unpopular word, *serving* each other, are less and less available as mothers and fathers seek their independent destinies outside the family.   43

As for love of children, this love is increasingly expressed through   44
supplying material comforts, amusements, and educational opportunities. Parents show their love for their children by sending them to
good schools and camps, by providing them with good food and good
doctors, by buying them toys, books, games, and a television set of
their very own. Parents will even go further and express their love by
attending PTA meetings to improve their children's schools, or by join-
ing groups that are acting to improve the quality of their children's television programs.

But this is love at a remove, and is rarely understood by children.   45
The more direct forms of parental love require time and patience,
steady, dependable, ungrudgingly given time actually spent *with* children, reading to them, comforting them, playing, joking, and working
with them. But even if parents were eager and willing to demonstrate
that sort of direct love to their children today, the opportunities are
diminished. What with school and Little League and piano lessons
and of course, the inevitable television programs, a day seems to offer
just enough time for a good-night kiss.

QUESTIONS FOR DISCUSSION

1   According to Winn, in what ways were the early predictions of the
    impact of television on family life mistaken?

2   Does the disturbing picture Winn presents of families coming
    home to a world of total immersion in television seem represen-
    tative to you, or extreme?

3   Why does Winn believe that television has eroded family rituals
    and created a sameness in family lifestyles? What reasoning and
    facts does she provide to back up her ideas?

4   Why does Winn believe that television makes it difficult for people
    to maintain meaningful, empathetic relationships?

5   According to Winn, how does television perpetuate "an unsatis-
    factory *status quo*"?

IDEAS FOR WRITING

1   Write an essay in which you compare a family that watches little
    or no television with a family of heavy television viewers. What
    differences do you notice in the frequency of ritual activities such
    as common meals and games in comparing these families?

2   Write an essay in which you evaluate Winn's central hypothesis. If
    you believe there are other causes of the erosion of family rituals
    and traditions than the pervasiveness of television, identify them.

Aggression: The Impact of Media Violence

SISSELA BOK

Sissela Bok has made a major contribution to the contemporary debate over values and ethical issues such as lying, euthanasia, peace, and the impact of mass media on society. Born in Sweden in 1934 to liberal economists and peace activists Alva and Gunnar Myrdal, Bok was influenced by her parents' devotion to public causes; in 1992 she wrote a biography of her mother, Alva Myrdal: A Daughter's Memoir. *Bok left Sweden at an early age to study abroad; she received her Ph.D. in philosophy from Harvard University in 1970. She has been a professor of philosophy at Brandeis University and is currently a Distinguished Fellow at the Harvard Center for Population and Development Studies. Bok's writings on ethical issues include* Lying: Moral Choice in Public and Private Life *(1978),* Secrets: On the Ethics of Concealment and Revelation *(1983),* A Strategy for Peace: Human Values and the Threat of War *(1989),* Common Values *(1995), and, most recently,* Mayhem: Violence as Public Entertainment *(1998), which contains the following essay on the relationship between media and aggression. Although she believes that media violence has a negative impact on children and society, Bok wishes to avoid simplistic solutions and finger pointing; she perceives relationships between media and violence as complex phenomena deserving of careful, reasoned analysis.*

Even if media violence were linked to no other debilitating effects, it would remain at the center of public debate so long as the widespread belief persists that it glamorizes aggressive conduct, removes inhibitions toward such conduct, arouses viewers, and invites imitation. It is only natural that the links of media violence to aggression should be of special concern to families and communities. Whereas increased fear, desensitization, and appetite primarily affect the viewers themselves, aggression directly injures others and represents a more clear-cut violation of standards of behavior. From the point of view of public policy, therefore, curbing aggression has priority over alleviating subtler psychological and moral damage.

Public concern about a possible link between media violence and societal violence has further intensified in the past decade, as violent crime reached a peak in the early 1990s, yet has shown no sign of downturn, even after crime rates began dropping in 1992. Media coverage of violence, far from declining, has escalated since then, devoting ever more attention to celebrity homicides and copycat crimes. The latter, explicitly modeled on videos or films and sometimes carried out with meticulous fidelity to detail, are never more relentlessly covered in the media than when they are committed by children and adolescents. Undocumented claims that violent copycat crimes are mounting in number contribute further to the ominous sense of threat that these crimes generate. Their dramatic nature drains away the public's attention from other, more mundane forms of aggression that are much more commonplace, and from . . . other . . . harmful effects of media violence.

Media analyst Ken Auletta reports that, in 1992, a mother in France   3
sued the head of a state TV channel that carried the American series *MacGyver,* claiming that her son was accidentally injured as a result of having copied MacGyver's recipe for making a bomb. At the time, Auletta predicted that similar lawsuits were bound to become a weapon against media violence in America's litigious culture. By 1996, novelist John Grisham had sparked a debate about director Oliver Stone's film *Natural Born Killers,* which is reputedly linked to more copycat assaults and murders than any other movie to date. Grisham wrote in protest against the film after learning that a friend of his, Bill Savage, had been killed by nineteen-year-old Sarah Edmondson and her boyfriend Benjamin Darras, eighteen: after repeated viewings of Stone's film on video, the two had gone on a killing spree with the film's murderous, gleeful heroes expressly in mind. Characterizing the film as "a horrific movie that glamorized casual mayhem and blood-lust," Grisham proposed legal action:

> Think of a film as a product, something created and brought to market, not too dissimilar from breast implants. Though the law has yet to declare movies to be products, it is only a small step away. If something goes wrong with the product, either by design or defect, and injury ensues, then its makers are held responsible. . . . It will take only one large ver-dict against the like of Oliver Stone, and his production company, and perhaps the screenwriter, and the studio itself, and then the party will be over. The verdict will come from the heartland, far away from Southern California, in some small courtroom with no cameras. A jury will finally say enough is enough; that the demons placed in Sarah Edmondson's mind were not solely of her own making.

As a producer of books made into lucrative movies—themselves   4
hardly devoid of violence—and as a veteran of contract negotiations within the entertainment industry, Grisham may have become accustomed to thinking of films in industry terms as "products." As a seasoned courtroom lawyer, he may have found the analogy between such products and breast implants useful for invoking product liability to pin personal responsibility on movie producers and directors for the lethal consequences that their work might help unleash.

Oliver Stone retorted that Grisham was drawing "upon the super-   5
stition about the magical power of pictures to conjure up the undead

spectre of censorship." In dismissing concerns about the "magical power of pictures" as merely superstitious, Stone sidestepped the larger question of responsibility fully as much as Grisham had sidestepped that of causation when he attributed liability to filmmakers for anything that "goes wrong" with their products so that "injury ensues."

Because aggression is the most prominent effect associated with media violence in the public's mind, it is natural that it should also remain the primary focus of scholars in the field. The "aggressor effect" has been studied both to identify the short-term, immediate impact on viewers after exposure to TV violence, and the long-term influences. . . . There is near-unanimity by now among investigators that exposure to media violence contributes to lowering barriers to aggression among some viewers. This lowering of barriers may be assisted by the failure of empathy that comes with growing desensitization, and intensified to the extent that viewers develop an appetite for violence—something that may lead to still greater desire for violent programs and, in turn, even greater desensitization.   6

When it comes to viewing violent pornography, levels of aggression toward women have been shown to go up among male subjects who view sexualized violence against women. "In explicit depictions of sexual violence," a report by the American Psychological Association's Commission on Youth and Violence concludes after surveying available research data, "it is the message about violence more than the sexual nature of the materials that appears to affect the attitudes of adolescents about rape and violence toward women." Psychologist Edward Donnerstein and colleagues have shown that if investigators tell subjects that aggression is legitimate, then show them violent pornography, their aggression toward women increases. In slasher films, the speed and ease with which "one's feelings can be transformed from sensuality into viciousness may surprise even those quite conversant with the links between sexual and violent urges."   7

Viewers who become accustomed to seeing violence as an acceptable, common, attractive way of dealing with problems find it easier to identify with aggressors and to suppress any sense of pity or respect for victims of violence. Media violence has been found to have stronger effects of this kind when carried out by heroic, impressive, or otherwise exciting figures, especially when they are shown as invulnerable and are rewarded or not punished for what they do. The same is true when the violence is shown as justifiable, when viewers identify with the aggressors rather than with their victims, when violence is routinely resorted to, and when the programs have links to how viewers perceive their own environment.   8

While the consensus that such influences exist grows among investigators as research accumulates, there is no consensus whatsoever about the size of the correlations involved. Most investigators agree that it will always be difficult to disentangle the precise effects of   9 exposure to media violence from the many other factors contributing to societal violence. No reputable scholar accepts the view expressed by 21 percent of the American public in 1995, blaming television more than any other factor for teenage violence. Such tentative estimates as have been made suggest that the media account for between 5 and 15 percent of societal violence. Even these estimates are rarely specific enough to indicate whether what is at issue is all violent crime, or such crimes along with bullying and aggression more generally.

One frequently cited investigator proposes a dramatically higher and more specific estimate than others. Psychiatrist Brandon S. Centerwall has concluded from large-scale epidemiological studies of "white homicide" in the United States, Canada, and South Africa in the period from 1945 to 1974, that it escalated in these societies within ten to fifteen years of the introduction of television, and that one can therefore deduce that television has brought a doubling of violent societal crime: 10

> Of course, there are many factors other than television that influence the amount of violent crime. Every violent act is the result of a variety of forces coming together—poverty, crime, alcohol and drug abuse, stress—of which childhood TV exposure is just one. Nevertheless, the evidence indicates that if hypothetically, television technology had never been developed, there would today be 10,000 fewer homicides each year in the United States, 70,000 fewer rapes, and 700,000 fewer injurious assaults. Violent crime would be half of what it now is.

Centerwall's study, published in 1989, includes controls for such variables as firearm possession and economic growth. But his conclusions have been criticized for not taking into account other factors, such as population changes during the time period studied, that might also play a role in changing crime rates. Shifts in policy and length of prison terms clearly affect these levels as well. By now, the decline in levels of violent crime in the United States since Centerwall's study was conducted, even though television viewing did not decline ten to fifteen years before, does not square with his extrapolations. As for "white homicide" in South Africa under apartheid, each year brings more severe challenges to official statistics from that period. 11

Even the lower estimates, however, of around 5 to 10 percent of violence as correlated with television exposure, point to substantial numbers of violent crimes in a population as large as America's. But if such estimates are to be used in discussions of policy decisions, more research will be needed to distinguish between the effects of television in general and those of particular types of violent programming, and to indicate specifically what sorts of images increase the aggressor effect and by what means; and throughout to be clearer about the nature of the aggressive acts studied. 12

Media representatives naturally request proof of such effects before they are asked to undertake substantial changes in programming. 13

In considering possible remedies for a problem, inquiring into the reasons for claims about risks is entirely appropriate. It is clearly valid to scrutinize the research designs, sampling methods, and possible biases of studies supporting such claims, and to ask about the reasoning leading from particular research findings to conclusions. But to ask for some demonstrable pinpointing of just when and how exposure to media violence affects levels of aggression sets a dangerously high threshold for establishing risk factors.

We may never be able to trace, retrospectively, the specific set of   14
television programs that contributed to a particular person's aggressive conduct. The same is true when it comes to the links between tobacco smoking and cancer, between drunk driving and automobile accidents, and many other risk factors presenting public health hazards. Only recently have scientists identified the specific channels through which tobacco generates its carcinogenic effects. Both precise causative mechanisms and documented occurrences in individuals remain elusive. Too often, media representatives formulate their requests in what appear to be strictly polemical terms, raising dismissive questions familiar from debates over the effects of tobacco: "How can anyone definitively pinpoint the link between media violence and acts of real-life violence? If not, how can we know if exposure to media violence constitutes a risk factor in the first place?"

Yet the difficulty in carrying out such pinpointing has not stood in   15
the way of discussing and promoting efforts to curtail cigarette smoking and drunk driving. It is not clear, therefore, why a similar difficulty should block such efforts when it comes to media violence. The perspective of "probabilistic causation" . . . is crucial to public debate about the risk factors in media violence. The television industry has already been persuaded to curtail the glamorization of smoking and drunk driving on its programs, despite the lack of conclusive documentation of the correlation between TV viewing and higher incidence of such conduct. Why should the industry not take analogous precautions with respect to violent programming?

Americans have special reasons to inquire into the causes of soci-   16
etal violence. While we are in no sense uniquely violent, we need to ask about all possible reasons why our levels of violent crime are higher than in all other stable industrialized democracies. Our homicide rate would be higher still if we did not imprison more of our citizens than any society in the world, and if emergency medical care had not improved so greatly in recent decades that a larger proportion of shooting victims survive than in the past. Even so, we have seen an unprecedented rise not only in child and adolescent violence, but in levels of rape, child abuse, domestic violence, and every other form of assault.

Although America's homicide rate has declined in the 1990s, the   17
rates for suicide, rape, and murder involving children and adolescents

in many regions have too rarely followed suit. For Americans aged 15 to 35 years, homicide is the second leading cause of death, and for young African Americans, 15 to 24 years, it is *the* leading cause of death. In the decade following the mid-1980s, the rate of murder committed by teenagers 14 to 17 more than doubled. The rates of injury suffered by small children are skyrocketing, with the number of seriously injured children nearly quadrupling from 1986 to 1993; and a proportion of these injuries are inflicted by children upon one another. Even homicides by children, once next to unknown, have escalated in recent decades.

America may be the only society on earth to have experienced what   18 has been called an "epidemic of children killing children," which is ravaging some of its communities today. As in any epidemic, it is urgent to ask what it is that makes so many capable of such violence, victimizes so many others, and causes countless more to live in fear. Whatever role the media are found to play in this respect, to be sure, is but part of the problem. Obviously, not even the total elimination of media violence would wipe out the problem of violence in the United States or any other society. The same can be said for the proliferation and easy access to guns, or for poverty, drug addiction, and other risk factors. As Dr. Deborah Prothrow-Stith puts it, "It's not an either or. It's not guns or media or parents or poverty."

We have all witnessed the four effects that I have discussed . . . —   19 fearfulness, numbing, appetite, and aggressive impulses—in the context of many influences apart from the media. Maturing involves learning to resist the dominion that these effects can gain over us; and to strive, instead, for greater resilience, empathy, self-control, and respect for self and others. The process of maturation and growth in these respects is never completed for any of us; but it is most easily thwarted in childhood, before it has had chance to take root. Such learning calls for nurturing and education at first; then for increasing autonomy in making personal decisions about how best to confront the realities of violence.

Today, the sights and sounds of violence on the screen affect this   20 learning process from infancy on, in many homes. The television screen is the lens through which most children learn about violence. Through the magnifying power of this lens, their everyday life becomes suffused by images of shootings, family violence, gang warfare, kidnappings, and everything else that contributes to violence in our society. It shapes their experiences long before they have had the opportunity to consent to such shaping or developed the ability to cope adequately with this knowledge. The basic nurturing and protection to prevent the impairment of this ability ought to be the birthright of every child.

QUESTIONS FOR DISCUSSION

1   What question does Bok believe John Grisham and Oliver Stone sidestep in their debate over the impact of films on "copycat" violent crimes? Do their arguments seem reasonable to you?

2   According to the research that Bok discusses, what circumstances seem to have the greatest impact on viewers' tendency to find violence acceptable? What further research remains to be done, in Bok's view, before we can draw more definitive conclusions about the impact of such violence on actual patterns of aggression?

3   Bok notes the difficulty in pointing to a clear-cut connection between smoking and cancer, although we presume there is a cause. How effective is her analogy with media violence as a presumed cause of actual violence among heavy viewers? Do her conclusions here seem clear and reasonable?

4   What does Dr. Deborah Prothrow-Stith mean when she states, "It's not an either or. It's not guns or media or parents or poverty"? What conclusions does Bok suggest can be drawn from this statement about causes and solutions for the problem of media violence?

5   How, according to Bok, might excessive exposure to media violence thwart a child's ability to learn to resist aggression and acquire such traits as empathy, respect, and self-control? Do you agree?

QUESTIONS FOR WRITING

1   Write an essay in which you compare the views on the impact of television violence on youth contained in Bok's essay with those in the next essay, Mike Males's "Who Us? Stop Blaming Kids and TV." Whose position do you find clearer and more convincing?

2   Although she is convinced that media violence has a negative impact on children's maturation, Bok points out the difficulty of collecting accurate statistics and drawing clear-cut causal relations in this area. Write about some ideas for research studies that you would like to see conducted that would give convincing evidence of such media-related causes and effects.

Who Us? Stop Blaming Kids and TV

MIKE MALES

Mike Males (b. 1950), currently a Ph.D. student and teaching assistant in the School of Social Ecology at the University of California, Irvine, received a B.A. in political science in 1972 from Occidental College in Los Angeles. Males lived for many years in Montana, where he worked with organizations such as the Youth Conservation Corps, served as a recreation leader and advocate for abused and neglected youth, and did research on youth smoking problems for the American Cancer Society. Males has been a contributor to many journals, including Western Criminology Review, *the* Lancet, *and the* Journal of Public Health Policy. *He has published two recent books,* The Scapegoat Generation: America's War on Adolescents *(1996) and* Ten Myths About the New Generation *(1998), both of which focus on the blaming of teens and the mass media for problems such as youth violence and teen sex, problems that Males believes stem from neglect, violence, and abuse by parents and other adults rather than from advertisements and violent, sex-oriented media programming.*

"Children have never been very good at listening to their elders," 1
James Baldwin wrote in *Nobody Knows My Name.* "But they have never failed to imitate them." This basic truth has all but disappeared as the public increasingly treats teenagers as a robot-like population under sway of an exploitative media. White House officials lecture film, music, Internet, fashion, and pop-culture moguls and accuse them of programming kids to smoke, drink, shoot up, have sex, and kill.

So do conservatives, led by William Bennett and Dan Quayle. Pro- 2
fessional organizations are also into media-bashing. In its famous report on youth risks, the Carnegie Corporation devoted a full chapter to media influences.

Progressives are no exception. *Mother Jones* claims it has "proof 3
that TV makes kids violent." And the Institute of Alternative Media emphasizes, "the average American child will witness . . . 200,000 acts of (TV) violence" by the time that child graduates from high school.

None of these varied interests note that during the eighteen years 4
between a child's birth and graduation from high school, there will be fifteen million cases of *real* violence in American homes grave enough to require hospital emergency treatment. These assaults will cause ten million serious injuries and 40,000 deaths to children. In October 1996, the Department of Health and Human Services reported 565,000 serious injuries that abusive parents inflicted on children and youths in 1993. The number is up four-fold since 1986.

The Department of Health report disappeared from the news 5
in one day. It elicited virtually no comment from the White House,

Republicans, or law-enforcement officials. Nor from Carnegie scholars, whose 150-page study, "Great Transitions: Preparing Adolescents for a New Century," devotes two sentences to household violence. The left press took no particular interest in the story, either.

All sides seem to agree that fictional violence, sex on the screen, Joe 6
Camel, beer-drinking frogs, or naked bodies on the Internet pose a bigger threat to children than do actual beatings, rape, or parental addictions. This, in turn, upholds the Clinton doctrine that youth behavior is the problem, and curbing young people's rights the answer.

Claims that TV causes violence bear little relation to real behavior. 7
Japanese and European kids behold media as graphically brutal as that which appears on American screens, but seventeen-year-olds in those countries commit murder at rates lower than those of American seventy-year-olds.

Likewise, youths in different parts of the United States are exposed 8
to the same media but display drastically different violence levels. TV violence does not account for the fact that the murder rate among black teens in Washington, D.C., is twenty-five times higher than that of white teens living a few Metro stops away. It doesn't explain why, nationally, murder doubled among nonwhite and Latino youth over the last decade, but declined among white Anglo teens. Furthermore, contrary to the TV brainwashing theory, Anglo sixteen-year-olds have lower violent-crime rates than black sixty-year-olds, Latino forty-year-olds, and Anglo thirty-year-olds. Men, women, whites, Latino, blacks, Asians, teens, young adults, middle-agers, and senior citizens in Fresno County—California's poorest urban area—display murder and violent-crime rates double those of their counterparts in Ventura County, the state's richest.

Confounding every theory, America's biggest explosion in felony vio- 9
lent crime is not street crime among minorities or teens of any color, but domestic violence among aging, mostly white baby boomers. Should we arm Junior with a V-chip to protect him from Mom and Dad?

In practical terms, media-violence theories are not about kids, but 10
about race and class: If TV accounts for any meaningful fraction of murder levels among poorer, nonwhite youth, why doesn't it have the same effect on white kids? Are minorities inherently programmable?

The newest target is Channel One, legitimately criticized by the 11
Unplug Campaign—a watchdog sponsored by the Center for Commercial-Free Public Education—as a corporate marketing ploy packaged as educational TV. But then the Unplug Campaign gives credence to claims that "commercials control kids" by "harvesting minds," as Roy Fox of the University of Missouri says. These claims imply that teens are uniquely open to media brainwashing.

Other misleading claims come from Johns Hopkins University 12
media analyst Mark Crispin Miller. In his critique of Channel One in the May edition of *Extra!*, Miller invoked such hackneyed phrases as

the "inevitable rebelliousness of adolescent boys," the "hormones raging," and the "defiant boorish behavior" of "young men." Despite the popularity of these stereotypes, there is no basis in fact for such anti-youth bias.

A 1988 study in the *Journal of Youth and Adolescence* by psychology   13
professors Grayson Holmbeck and John Hill concluded: "Adolescents are *not* in turmoil, *not* deeply disturbed, *not* at the mercy of their impulses, *not* resistant to parental values, and *not* rebellious."

In the November 1992 *Journal of the American Academy of Child*   14
and Adolescent Psychiatry, Northwestern University psychiatry professor Daniel Offer reviewed 150 studies and concluded, in his article "Debunking the Myths of Adolescence," that "the effects of pubertal hormones are neither potent nor pervasive."

If anything, Channel One and other mainstream media reinforce   15
young people's conformity to—not defiance of—adult values. Miller's unsubstantiated claims that student consumerism, bad behaviors, and mental or biological imbalances are compelled by media ads and images could be made with equal force about the behaviors of his own age group. Binge drinking, drug abuse, and violence against children by adults over the age of thirty are rising rapidly.

The barrage of sexually seductive liquor ads, fashion images, and   16
anti-youth rhetoric, by conventional logic, must be influencing those hormonally unstable middle-agers.

I worked for a dozen years in youth programs in Montana and Cal-   17
ifornia. When problems arose, they usually crossed generations. I saw violent kids with dads or uncles in jail for assault. I saw middle-schoolers molested in childhood by mom's boyfriend. I saw budding teen alcoholics hoisting forty-ounces alongside forty-year-old sots. I also saw again and again how kids start to smoke. In countless trailers and small apartments dense with blue haze, children roamed the rugs as grownups puffed. Mom and seventh-grade daughter swapped Dorals while bemoaning the evils of men. A junior-high basketball center slept outside before a big game because a dozen elders—from her non-inhaling sixteen-year-old brother to her grandma—were all chain smokers. Two years later, she'd given up and joined the party.

As a rule, teen smoking mimicked adult smoking by gender, race,   18
locale, era, and household. I could discern no pop-culture puppetry. My survey of 400 Los Angeles middle schoolers for a 1994 *Journal of School Health* article found children of smoking parents three times more likely to smoke by age fifteen than children of non-smokers. Parents were the most influential but not the only adults kids emulated. Nor did youngsters copy elders slavishly. Youths often picked slightly different habits (like chewing tobacco, or their own brands).

In 1989, the Centers for Disease Control lamented, "75 percent of   19
all teenage smokers come from homes where parents smoke." You don't hear such candor from today's put-politics-first health agencies.

Centers for Disease Control tobacco chieftain Michael Eriksen informed me that his agency doesn't make an issue of parental smoking. Nor do anti-smoking groups. Asked Kathy Mulvey, research director of INFACT: "Why make enemies of fifty million adult smokers" when advertising creates the real "appeal of tobacco to youth?"

Do ads hook kids on cigarettes? Studies of the effects of the Joe   20
Camel logo show only that a larger fraction of teen smokers than veteran adult smokers choose the Camel brand. When asked, some researchers admit they cannot demonstrate that advertising causes kids to smoke who would not otherwise. And that's the real issue. In fact, surveys found smoking declining among teens (especially the youngest) during Joe's advent from 1985 to 1990.

The University of California's Stanton Glantz, whose exposure of   21
10,000 tobacco documents enraged the industry, found corporate perfidy far shrewder than camels and cowboys.

"As the tobacco industry knows well," Glantz reported, "kids want   22
to be like adults." An industry marketing document advises: "To reach young smokers, present the cigarette as one of the initiations into adult life . . . the basic symbols of growing up."

The biggest predictor of whether a teen will become a smoker, a   23
drunk, or a druggie is whether or not the child grows up amid adult addicts. Three-fourths of murdered kids are killed by adults. Suicide and murder rates among white teenagers resemble those of white adults, and suicide and murder rates among black teens track those of black adults. And as far as teen pregnancy goes, for minor mothers, four-fifths of the fathers are adults over eighteen, and half are adults over twenty.

The inescapable conclusion is this: If you want to change juvenile   24
behavior, change adult behavior. But instead of focusing on adults, almost everyone points a finger at kids—and at the TV culture that supposedly addicts them.

Groups like Mothers Against Drunk Driving charge, for instance,   25
that Budweiser's frogs entice teens to drink. Yet the 1995 National Household Survey found teen alcohol use declining. "Youths aren't buying the cute and flashy beer images," an in-depth *USA Today* survey found. Most teens found the ads amusing, but they did not consume Bud as a result.

By squabbling over frogs, political interests can sidestep the im-   26
politic tragedy that adults over the age of twenty-one cause 90 percent of America's 16,000 alcohol-related traffic deaths every year. Clinton and drug-policy chief Barry McCaffrey ignore federal reports that show a skyrocketing toll of booze and drug-related casualties among adults in their thirties and forties—the age group that is parenting most American teens. But both officials get favorable press attention by blaming alcohol ads and heroin chic for corrupting our kids.

Progressive reformers who insist kids are so malleable that beer frogs   27
and Joe Camel and Ace Ventura push them to evil are not so different

from those on the Christian right who claim that *Our Bodies, Ourselves* promotes teen sex and that the group Rage Against the Machine persuades pubescents to roll down Rodeo Drive with a shotgun.

America's increasingly marginalized young deserve better than grownup escapism. Millions of children and teenagers face real destitution, drug abuse, and violence in their homes. Yet these profound menaces continue to lurk in the background, even as the frogs, V-chips, and Mighty Morphins take center stage. 28

QUESTIONS FOR DISCUSSION

1 In what sense could the quotation from Baldwin's *Nobody Knows My Name* at the start of this essay be considered the thesis for it?

2 One strategy that Males uses in his essay is that of contrasting statistics. Give examples of how the contrasts he establishes between several sets of statistics help him make his point about the real causes of teen violence and substance abuse.

3 In addition to pointing out what he believes to be the true causes of teen misbehavior, Males suggests alternative solutions to the underlying problems. In contrast to the "progressive reformers" who wish to censor the media and advertisements, what kind of social reforms does he seem to be proposing?

4 How does Males use his own personal observations and surveying of youth smokers to refute the idea that cigarette ads lead children to smoke? Are his arguments convincing?

5 Give examples of emotional language and sarcasm in Males's essay. Does his use of such language add to or detract from the effectiveness of his argument?

QUESTIONS FOR WRITING

1 Write a response to Males's essay in which you focus on his argument that adults, rather than the media, are to blame for teen violence and substance abuse. Does it follow that it is pointless to try to control media depictions of drug and alcohol use, sex, and violence in fictional programming and in advertising?

2 Assuming that Males is correct that adult patterns of irresponsibility and abuse lead to similar patterns of abuse among teenagers, write an essay describing how you would design an effective ad campaign targeted at adult viewers that would encourage them to understand the impact of such behavior on young people. If you have seen such ads on television or in other media outlets, you might provide examples.

Men, Women, and Computers

BARBARA KANTROWITZ

Barbara Kantrowitz has been a writer and editor for Newsweek *since 1985. She has written on early childhood education, the development of ethics and morality in children, youth violence and its roots in child abuse, and the resurgence of spirituality in American life. In the following selection, Kantrowitz argues that men dominate on-line interactions and proposes some solutions to the alienation from technology that many women experience today.*

As a longtime "Star Trek" devotee, Janis Cortese was eager to be part   1
of the Trekkie discussion group on the Internet. But when she first logged on, Cortese noticed that these fans of the final frontier devoted megabytes to such profound topics as whether Troi or Crusher had bigger breasts. In other words, the purveyors of this "Trek" dreck were all *guys*. Undeterred, Cortese, a physicist at California's Loma Linda University, figured she'd add her perspective to the electronic gathering place with her own momentous questions. Why was the male cast racially diverse while almost all the females were young, white and skinny? Then, she tossed in a few lustful thoughts about the male crew members.

After those seemingly innocuous observations, "I was chased off   2
the net by rabid hounds," recalls Cortese. Before she could say "Fire phasers," the Trekkies had flooded her electronic mailbox with nasty messages—a practice called "flaming." Cortese retreated into her own galaxy by starting the all-female Starfleet Ladies Auxiliary and Embroidery/Baking Society. The private electronic forum, based in Houston, now has more than 40 members, including psychologists, physicians, students and secretaries. They started with Trektalk, but often chose to beam down and go where no man had ever wandered before—into the personal mode. When Julia Kosatka, a Houston computer scientist, got pregnant last year, she shared her thoughts with the group on weight gain, sex while expecting and everything else on her mind. Says Kosatka: "I'm part of one of the longest-running slumber parties in history."

From the Internet, to Silicon Valley to the PC sitting in the family   3
room, men and women often seem like two chips that pass in the night. Sure, there are women who spout techno-speak in their sleep and plenty of men who think a hard drive means four hours on the freeway. But in general, computer culture is created, defined and controlled by men. Women often feel about as welcome as a system crash.

About a third of American families have at least one computer, but   4
most of those are purchased and used by males. It may be new technology, but the old rules still apply. In part, it's that male-machine

bonding thing, reincarnated in the digital age. "Men tend to be seduced by the technology itself," says Oliver Strimpel, executive director of The Computer Museum in Boston. "They tend to get into the faster-race-car syndrome," bragging about the size of their discs or the speed of their microprocessors. To the truly besotted, computers are a virtual religion, complete with icons (on-screen graphics), relics (obsolete programs and machines) and prophets (Microsoft's Bill Gates, outlaw hackers). This is not something to be trifled with by mere . . . females, who seem to think that machines were meant to be *used*, like the microwave oven or the dishwasher. Interesting and convenient on the job but not worthy of obsession. Esther Dyson, editor of Release 1.0, an influential software-industry newsletter, has been following the computer field for two decades. Yet when she looks at her own computer, Dyson says she still doesn't "really care about its innards. I just want it to work."

Blame (a) culture (b) family (c) schools (d) all of the above. Little   5
boys are expected to roll around in the dirt and explore. Perfect training for learning to use computers, which often requires hours in front of the screen trying to figure out the messy arcanum of a particular program. Girls get subtle messages—from society if not from their parents—that they should keep their hands clean and play with their dolls. Too, often, they're discouraged from taking science and math— not just by their schools but by parents as well (how many mothers have patted their daughters on the head and reassured them: "Oh, I wasn't good at math, either").

The gender gap is real and takes many forms.   6

Barbie vs. Nintendo

Girls' technophobia begins early. Last summer, Sarah Douglas, a   7
University of Oregon computer-science professor, took part in a job fair for teenage girls that was supposed to introduce them to nontraditional occupations. With great expectations, she set up her computer and loaded it with interesting programs. Not a single girl stopped by. When she asked why, the girls "told me computers were something their dads and their brothers used," Douglas sadly recalls. "Computer science is a very male profession. . . . When girls get involved in that male world, they are pushed away and belittled. Pretty soon, the girls get frustrated and drop out."

Computer games usually involve lots of shooting and dying. Boy   8
stuff. What's out there for girls? "If you walk down the street and look in the computer store, you will see primarily male people as sales staff and as customers," says Jo Sanders, director of the gender-equity program at the Center for Advanced Study in Education at the City University of New York Graduate Center.

Boys and girls are equally interested in computers until about the   9
fifth grade, says University of Minnesota sociologist Ronald Anderson,
who coauthored the recent report "Computers in American Schools."
At that point, boys' use rises significantly and girls' use drops, Anderson says, probably because sex-role identification really kicks in. Many
girls quickly put computers on the list of not-quite-feminine topics,
like car engines and baseball batting averages. It didn't have to be this
way. The very first computer programmer was a woman, Ada Lovelace,
who worked with Charles Babbage on his mechanical computing
machines in the mid-1800s. If she had become a role model, maybe
hundreds of thousands of girls would have spent their teenage years
locked in their bedrooms staring at screens. Instead, too many are
doing their nails or worrying about their hair, says Marcelline Barron,
an administrator at the Illinois Mathematics and Science Academy, a
publicly funded coed boarding school for gifted students. "You're not
thinking about calculus or physics when you're thinking about that,"
says Barron. "We have these kinds of expectations for young girls. They
must be neat, they must be clean, they must be quiet."

Despite great strides by women in other formerly male fields, such   10
as law and medicine, women are turning away from the computer
industry. Men earning computer-science degrees outnumber women
3 to 1 and the gap is growing, according to the National Science Foun-
dation. Fifteen years ago, when computers were still new in schools,
they hadn't yet been defined as so exclusively male. But now girls have
gotten the message. It's not just the technical and cultural barrier.
Sherry Turkle, a Massachusetts Institute of Technology sociologist
who teaches a course on women and computers, says that computers
have come to stand for "a world without emotion," an image that
seems to scare off girls more than boys.

In the past decade, videogames have become a gateway to tech-   11
nology for many boys, but game manufacturers say few girls are attracted to these small-screen shoot-'em-ups. It's not surprising that
the vast majority of videogame designers are men. They don't call it
Game *Boy* for nothing. Now some manufacturers are trying to lure
girls. In the next few months, Sega plans to introduce "Berenstein
Bears," which will offer players a choice of boy or girl characters. A
second game, "Crystal's Pony Tale," involves coloring (there's lots of
pink in the background). Neither game requires players to "die," a
common videogame device that researchers say girls dislike. Girls also
tend to prefer nonlinear games, where there is more than one way to
proceed. "There's a whole issue with speaking girls' language," says
Michealene Cristini Risley, group director of licensing and character
development for Sega. The company would like to hook girls at the
age of 4, before they've developed fears of technology.

Girls need freedom to explore and make mistakes. Betsy Zeller, a   12
37-year-old engineering manager at Silicon Graphics, says that when

she discovered computers in college, "I swear I thought I'd seen the face of God." Yet she had to fend off guys who would come into the lab and want to help her work through problems or, worse yet, do them for her. "I would tell them to get lost," she says. "I wanted to do it myself." Most women either asked for or accepted proffered help, just as they are more likely to ask for directions when lost in a strange city. That may be the best way to avoid driving in circles for hours, but it's not the best way to learn technical subjects.

Schools are trying a number of approaches to interest girls in computers. Douglas and her colleagues are participating in a mentorship program where undergraduate girls spend a summer working with female computer scientists. Studies have shown that girls are more attracted to technology if they can work in groups; some schools are experimenting with team projects that require computers but are focused on putting out a product, like a newspaper or pamphlet. At the middle- and high-school level, girls-only computer classes are increasingly popular. Two months ago Roosevelt Middle School in Eugene, Ore., set up girls-only hours at the computer lab. Games were prohibited and artists were brought in to teach girls how to be more creative with the computer. Students are also learning to use e-mail, which many girls love. Says Debbie Nehl, the computer-lab supervisor: "They see it as high-tech note-passing."   13

Power Networks

As a relatively new industry, the leadership of computerdom might be expected to be more gender-diverse. Wrong; few women have advanced beyond middle-management ranks. According to a study conducted last year by *The San Jose Mercury News,* there are no women CEOs [chief executive officers] running major computer-manufacturing firms and only a handful running software companies. Even women who have succeeded say they are acutely conscious of the differences between them and their male co-workers. "I don't talk the same as men," says Paula Hawthorn, an executive at Montage Software, in Oakland, Calif. "I don't get the same credibility." The difference, she says, "is with you all the time."   14

Women who work in very technical areas, such as programming, are·often the loneliest. Anita Borg, a computer-systems researcher, remembers attending a 1987 conference were there were so few women that the only time they ran into each other was in the restroom. Their main topic of discussion: why there were so few women at the conference. That bathroom cabal grew into Systers, an on-line network for women with technical careers. There are now 1,740 women members from 19 countries representing 200 colleges and universities and 150 companies. Systers is part mentoring and part   15 consciousness-raising. One graduate student, for example, talked about how uncomfortable she felt sitting in her shared office when a male graduate student and a professor put a picture of a nude woman on a computer. The problem was resolved when a couple of female faculty members, also on the Systers network, told their offending colleagues that the image was not acceptable.

Women have been more successful in developing software, especially when their focus is products used by children. Jan Davidson, a former teacher, started Davidson & Associates, in Torrance, Calif., with three programs in 1982. Now it's one of the country's biggest developers of kids' software, with 350 employees and $58.6 million in revenues. Multimedia will bring new opportunities for women. The technology is so specialized that it requires a team—animators, producers, scriptwriters, 3-D modelers—to create state-of-the-art products. It's a far cry from the stereotype of the solitary male programmer, laboring long into the night with only takeout Chinese food for company. At Mary Cron's Rymel Design Group in Palos Verdes, Calif., most of the software artists and designers are women, Cron says. "It's like a giant puzzle," she adds. "We like stuff we can work on together." 16

As more women develop software, they may also help create products that will attract women consumers—a huge untapped market. Heidi Roizen, a college English major, cofounded T/Maker Co. in Mountain View, Calif., a decade ago. She says that because women are often in charge of the family's budget, they are potential consumers of personal-finance programs. Women are also the most likely buyers of education and family-entertainment products, a fast-growing segment of the industry. "Women are more typically the household shopper," Roizen says. "They have tremendous buying power." 17

Wired Women

The infobahn—a.k.a. the Information Superhighway—may be the most hyped phenomenon in history—or it could be the road to the future. In any case, women want to get on. But the sign over the access road says CAUTION, MEN WORKING, WOMEN BEWARE. Despite hundreds of thousands of new users in the last year, men still dominate the Internet and commercial services such as Prodigy or CompuServe. The typical male conversation on line turns off many women. "A lot of time to be crude, it's a pissing contest," says Lisa Kimball, a partner in the Meta Network, a Washington, D. C. on-line service that is 40 percent female. Put-downs are an art form. When one woman complained recently in an Internet forum that she didn't like participating because she didn't have time to answer all her e-mail, she was swamped with angry responses, including this one (from a man): "Would you like some cheese with your whine?" 18

Some men say the on-line hostility comes from resentment over   19
women's slowly entering what has been an almost exclusively male
domain. Many male techno-jocks "Feel women are intruding into
their inner sanctum," says André Bacard, a Silicon Valley, Calif., technology writer. They're not out to win sensitivity contests. "In the computer world, it's 'Listen, baby, if you don't like it, drop dead,'" says
Bacard. "It's the way men talk to guys. Women aren't used to that."

Even under more civilized circumstances, men and women have   20
different conversational styles, says Susan Herring, a University of
Texas at Arlington professor who has studied women's participation on
computer networks. Herring found that violations of long-established
net etiquette—asking too many basic questions, for example—angered
men. "The women were much more tolerant of people who didn't
know what they were doing," Herring says. "What really annoyed
women was the flaming and people boasting. The things that annoy
women are things men do all the time."

Like hitting on women. Women have learned to tread their key-   21
boards carefully in chat forums because they often have to fend off
sexual advances that would make Bob Packwood blush. When subscribers to America Online enter one of the service's forums, their
computer names appear at the top of the screen as a kind of welcome.
If they've chosen an obviously female name, chances are they'll be
bombarded with private messages seeking detailed descriptions of
their appearance or sexual preferences. "I couldn't believe it," recalls
55-year-old Eva S. "I said, 'Come on, I'm a grandmother.'"

More and more women are signing on to networks that are either   22
coed and run by women, or are exclusively for women. Stacy Horn
started ECHO (for East Coast Hang Out) four years ago because she
was frustrated with the hostility on line. About 60 percent of ECHO's
2,000 subscribers are men; among ECHO's 50 forums, only two are
strictly for women. "Flaming is nonexistent on ECHO," Horn says.
"New women get on line and they see that. And then they're much
more likely to jump in." Women's Wire in San Francisco, started in
January, has 850 subscribers, only 10 percent of them men—the re-
verse of most on-line services. "We wanted to design a system in
which women would help shape the community and the rules of that
community from the floor up," says cofounder Ellen Pack. The official policy is that there is no such thing as a dumb question—and
no flaming.

Male subscribers say Women's Wire has been a learning experi-   23
ence for them, too. Maxwell Hoffmann, a 41-year-old computer company manager, says that many men think only women are overly
emotional. But men lose it, too. A typical on-line fight starts with
two guys sending "emotionally charged flames going back and forth"
through cyberspace (not on Women's Wire). Then it expands and

"everybody starts flaming the guy. They scream at each other and they're not listening."

If only men weren't so *emotional,* so *irrational,* could we all get along on the net?   24

Toys and Tools

In one intriguing study by the Center for Children and Technology, a New York think tank, men and women in technical fields were asked to dream up machines of the future. Men typically imagined devices that could help them "conquer the universe," says Jan Hawkins, director of the center. She says women wanted machines that met people's needs, "the perfect mother."   25

Someday, gender-blind education and socialization may render those differences obsolete. But in the meantime, researchers say both visions are useful. If everyone approached technology the way women do now, "we wouldn't be pushing envelopes," says Cornelia Bruner, associate director of the center. "Most women, even those who are technologically sophisticated, think of machines as a means to an end." Men think of the machines as an extension of their own power, as a way to "transcend physical limitations." That may be why they are more likely to come up with great leaps in technology, researchers say. Without that vision, the computer and its attendant industry would not exist.   26

Ironically, gender differences could help women. "We're at a cultural turning point," says MIT's Turkle. "There's an opportunity to remake the culture around the machine." Practicality is now as valued as invention. If the computer industry wants to put machines in the hands of the masses, that means women—along with the great many men who have no interest in hot-rod computing. An ad campaign for Compaq's popular Presario line emphasized the machine's utility. After kissing her child good night, the mother in the ad sits down at her Presario to work. As people start to view their machines as creative tools, someday women may be just as comfortable with computers as men are.   27

QUESTIONS FOR DISCUSSION

1   What led Janis Cortese to start her own private electronic forum? What need does the forum fill in the lives of its members?

2   According to Kantrowitz, how do men and women relate differently to their computers? Does she provide evidence for her views? Are her arguments convincing?

3   How are schools and video game designers trying to interest girls in computers? Do you think their efforts will be successful, or do

they seem to be motivated by misguided stereotypes of "feminine" thinking styles?

4   What is the purpose of the Systers on-line network? How does it
differ from Janis Cortese's forum? Does the Systers organization
seem to be effective, or could it be viewed as a form of withdrawal?

5   What does Kantrowitz perceive to be women's role in the future of
computing? How will women's contribution differ from the "great
leaps" of male computing innovators? Do you agree with her cate-
gorizations here?

IDEAS FOR WRITING

1   Write your own futuristic account of the role of women in computers. Do you agree with Kantrowitz's view, or do you think that
women will have a different role than she predicts?

2   Media critic Laura Miller has stated that although Kantrowitz
wants to protect women from the "Wild West" atmosphere of
cyberspace, women can fend for themselves and don't need "protection" in all-female chat groups. Write an essay in which you
respond to Miller's comment. Does her critique of Kantrowitz
seem fair and realistic? Why or why not?

Ethnicity and
Electronic Media

The Living Room

HENRY LOUIS GATES, JR.

Henry Louis Gates, Jr., (b. 1950), a leader in the educational reform movement known as multiculturalism, is a renowned scholar of African-American culture and the author of many books in the field. Gates, the son of a paper-factory worker, grew up in a small town in Virginia. He was admitted to Yale University, where he earned his B.A., and went on to Cambridge University, where he was the first African-American to receive a Ph.D. in English literature. Gates served as the director of African-American studies at Yale, Cornell, and Duke universities. Since 1991, he has held the W. E. B. Du Bois Professorship in the African-American Studies department at Harvard. Gates's books include The Signifying Monkey: A Theory of Afro-American Literary Criticism *(1988),* Loose Canons: Notes on the Culture Wars *(1992), and* Speaking of Race, Speaking of Sex: Hate Speech, Civil Rights, and Civil Liberties *(1994). In the following selection from his memoir,* Colored People *(1994), Gates describes the impact of television images of African-Americans on his family and community.*

When I was growing up in Piedmont, West Virginia, the TV was the ritual arena for the drama of race. In our family, it was located in the living room, where it functioned like a fireplace in the proverbial New England winter. I'd sit in the water in the galvanized tub in the middle of our kitchen, watching the TV in the next room while Mama did the laundry or some other chore as she waited for Daddy to come home from his second job. We watched people getting hosed and cracked over their heads, people being spat upon and arrested, rednecks siccing fierce dogs on women and children, our people responding by singing and marching and staying strong. Eyes on the prize. Eyes on the prize. George Wallace at the gate of the University of Alabama, blocking Autherine Lucy's way. Charlayne Hunter at the University of Georgia. President Kennedy interrupting our scheduled program with a special address, saying that James Meredith will *definitely* enter the University of Mississippi; and saying it like he believed it (unlike Ike), saying it like the big kids said "It's our turn to play" on the basketball court and walking all through us as if we weren't there. 1

The simple truth is that the civil rights era came late to Piedmont, even though it came early to our television set. We could watch what was going on Elsewhere on television, but the marches and sit-ins were as remote to us as, in other ways, was the all-colored world of *Amos and Andy*—a world full of black lawyers, black judges, black nurses, black doctors. 2

Politics aside, though, we were starved for images of ourselves and   3
searched TV to find them. Everybody, of course, watched sports, because Piedmont was a big sports town. Making the big leagues was
like getting to heaven, and everybody had hopes that they could, or a
relative could. We'd watch the games day and night, and listen on
radio to what we couldn't see. Everybody knew the latest scores, batting averages, rbi's, and stolen bases. Everybody knew the standings
in the leagues, who could still win the pennant and how. Everybody
liked the Dodgers because of Jackie Robinson, the same way everybody still voted Republican because of Abraham Lincoln. Sports on
the mind, sports in the mind. The only thing to rival the Valley in fascination was the big-league baseball diamond.

I once heard Mr. James Helms says, "You got to give the white man   4
his due when it comes to technology. One on one, though, and it's even-
steven. Joe Louis showed 'em that." We were obsessed with sports in
part because it was the only time we could compete with white people
even-steven. And the white people, it often seemed, were just as obsessed with this primal confrontation between the races as we were. I
think they integrated professional sports, after all those years of segregation, just to capitalize on this voyeuristic thrill of the forbidden contact. What interracial sex was to the seventies, interracial sports were to
the fifties. Except for sports, we rarely saw a colored person on TV.

Actually, I first got to know white people as "people" through their   5
flickering images on television shows. It was the television set that
brought us together at night, and the television set that brought in the
world outside the Valley. We were close enough to Washington to receive its twelve channels on cable. Piedmont was transformed from a
radio culture to one with the fullest range of television, literally
overnight. During my first-grade year, we'd watch *Superman, Lassie,*
Jack Benny, Danny Thomas, *Robin Hood, I Love Lucy, December Bride,*
Nat King Cole (of course), *Wyatt Earp, Broken Arrow,* Phil Silvers, Red
Skelton, *The $64,000 Question, Ozzie and Harriet, The Millionaire,*
Father Knows Best, The Lone Ranger, Bob Cummings, *Dragnet, The*
People's Choice, Rin Tin Tin, Jim Bowie, Gunsmoke, My Friend Flicka,
The Life of Riley, Topper, Dick Powell's Zane Grey Theater, Circus Boy,
and Loretta Young—all in prime time. My favorites were *The Life of*
Riley, in part because he worked in a factory like Daddy did, and *Ozzie*
and Harriet, in part because Ozzie never seemed to work at all. A year
later, however, *Leave It to Beaver* swept most of the others away.

With a show like *Topper,* I felt as if I was getting a glimpse, at last,   6
of the life that Mrs. Hudson, and Mrs. Thomas, and Mrs. Campbell
must be leading in their big mansions on East Hampshire Street.
Smoking jackets and cravats, spats and canes, elegant garden parties
and martinis. People who wore suits to eat dinner! This was a world
so elegantly distant from ours, it was like a voyage to another galaxy,
light-years away.

Leave It to Beaver, on the other hand, was a world much closer, but   7
just out of reach nonetheless. Beaver's street was where we wanted
to live, Beaver's house where we wanted to eat and sleep, Beaver's
father's firm where we'd have liked Daddy to work. These shows for us
were about property, the property that white people could own and
that we couldn't. About a level of comfort and ease at which we could
only wonder. It was the world that the integrated school was going to
prepare us to enter and that, for Mama, would be the prize.

If prime time consisted of images of middle-class white people who   8
looked nothing at all like us, late night was about the radio, listening to
Randy's Record Shop from Gallatin, Tennessee. My brother, Rocky, kept
a transistor radio by his bed, and he'd listen to it all night, for all I knew,
long after I'd fallen asleep. In 1956, black music hadn't yet broken
down into its many subgenres, except for large divisions such as jazz,
blues, gospel, rhythm and blues. On *Randy's,* you were as likely to hear
The Platters doing "The Great Pretender" and Clyde McPhatter doing
"Treasure of Love" as you were to hear Howlin' Wolf do "Smokestack
Lightning" or Joe Turner do "Corrine, Corrine." My own favorite that
year was the slow, deliberate sound of Jesse Belvin's "Goodnight, My
Love." I used to fall asleep singing it in my mind to my Uncle Earkie's
girlfriend Ula, who was a sweet caffe latte brown, with the blackest,
shiniest straight hair and the fullest, most rounded red lips. Not even
in your dreams, he had said to me one day, as I watched her red dress
slink down our front stairs. It was my first brush with the sublime.

We used to laugh at the way the disc jockey sang "Black Strap Lax-   9
a-teeves" during the commercials. I sometimes would wonder if the
kids we'd seen on TV in Little Rock or Birmingham earlier in the
evening were singing themselves to sleep with *their* Ulas.

Lord knows, we weren't going to learn how to be colored by watch-   10
ing television. Seeing somebody colored on TV was an event.

"Colored, colored, on Channel Two," you'd hear someone shout.   11
Somebody else would run to the phone, while yet another hit the front
porch, telling all the neighbors where to see it. And *everybody* loved
Amos and Andy—I don't care what people say today. For the colored
people, the day they took *Amos and Andy* off the air was one of the sad-
dest days in Piedmont, about as sad as the day of the last mill pic-a-nic.

What was special to us about *Amos and Andy* was that their world   12
was *all* colored, just like ours. Of course, *they* had their colored judges
and lawyers and doctors and nurses, which we could only dream
about having, or becoming—and we *did* dream about those things.
Kingfish ate his soft-boiled eggs delicately, out of an egg cup. He even
owned an acre of land in Westchester County, which he sold to Andy,
using the facade of a movie set to fake a mansion. As far as we were
concerned, the foibles of Kingfish or Calhoun the lawyer were the
foibles of individuals who happened to be funny. Nobody was likely to

confuse them with the colored people we knew, no more than we'd confuse ourselves with the entertainers and athletes we saw on TV or in *Ebony* or *Jet,* the magazines we devoured to keep up with what was happening with the race. And people took special relish in Kingfish's malapropisms. "I denies the allegation, Your Honor, and I resents the alligator."

In one of my favorite episodes of *Amos and Andy,* "The Punjab of Java-Pour," Andy Brown is hired to advertise a brand of coffee and is required to dress up as a turbaned Oriental potentate. Kingfish gets the bright idea that if he dresses up as a potentate's servant, the two of them can enjoy a vacation at a luxury hotel for free. So attired, the two promenade around the lobby, running up an enormous tab and generously dispensing "rubies" and "diamonds" as tips. The plan goes awry when people try to redeem the gems and discover them to be colored glass. It was widely suspected that this episode was what prompted two Negroes in Baltimore to dress like African princes and demand service in a segregated four-star restaurant. Once it was clear to the management that these were not American Negroes, the two were treated royally. When the two left the restaurant, they took off their African headdresses and robes and enjoyed a hearty laugh at the restaurant's expense. "They weren't like our Negroes," the maître d' told the press in explaining why he had agreed to seat the two "African princes."

Whenever the movies *Imitation of Life* and *The Green Pastures* would be shown on TV, we watched with similar hunger—especially *Imitation of Life.* It was never on early; only the late *late* show, like the performances of Cab Calloway and Duke Ellington at the Crystal Palace. And we'd stay up. Everybody colored. The men coming home on second shift from the paper mill would stay up. Those who had to go out on the day shift and who normally would have been in bed hours earlier (because they had to be at work at 6:30) would stay up. As would we, the kids, wired for the ritual at hand. And we'd all sit in silence, fighting back the tears, watching as Delilah invents the world's greatest pancakes and a down-and-out Ned Sparks takes one taste and says, flatly, "We'll box it." Cut to a big white house, plenty of money, and Delilah saying that she doesn't want her share of the money (which should have been *all* the money); she just wants to continue to cook, clean, wash, iron, and serve her good white lady and her daughter. (Nobody in our living room was going for *that.*) And then Delilah shows up at her light-complected daughter's school one day, unexpectedly, to pick her up, and there's the daughter, Peola, ducking down behind her books, and the white teacher saying, I'm sorry, ma'am, there must be some mistake. We have no little colored children here. And then Delilah, spying her baby, says, Oh, yes you do. Peola! Peola! Come here to your mammy, honey chile. And then Peola runs out of the room, breaking her poor, sweet mother's heart. And Peola continues to break her mother's heart, by passing, leaving the race, and marrying white. Yet her mama understands, always understands, and dying, makes detailed plans for her own big, beautiful funeral, complete with six white horses and a carriage and a jazz band, New Orleans style. And she dies and is about to be buried, when, out of nowhere, comes grown-up Peola, saying, "Don't die, Mama, don't die, Mama, I'm sorry, Mama, I'm sorry," and throws her light-and-bright-and-damn-near-white self onto her mama's casket. By this time, we have stopped trying to fight back the tears and are boo-hooing all over the place. Then we turn to our *own* mama and tell her how much we love her and swear that we will *never, ever* pass for white. I promise, Mama. I promise.

Peola had sold her soul to the Devil. This was the first popular Faust in the black tradition, the bargain with the Devil over the cultural soul. Talk about a cautionary tale.   15

The Green Pastures was an altogether more uplifting view of things, our Afro Paradiso. Make way for the Lawd! Make way for the Lawd! And Rex Ingram, dressed in a long black frock coat and a long white beard, comes walking down the Streets Paved with Gold, past the Pearly Gates, while Negroes with the whitest wings of fluffy cotton fly around heaven, playing harps, singing spirituals, having fish fries, and eating watermelon. Hard as I try, I can't stop seeing God as that black man who played Him in *The Green Pastures* and seeing Noah as Rochester from the Jack Benny show, trying to bargain with God to let him take along an extra keg of wine or two.   16

Civil rights took us all by surprise. Every night we'd wait until the news to see what "Dr. King and dem" were doing. It was like watching the Olympics or the World Series when somebody colored was on. The murder of Emmett Till was one of my first memories. He whistled at some white girl, they said; that's all he did. He was beat so bad they didn't even want to open the casket, but his mama made them. She wanted the world to see what they had done to her baby.   17

In 1957, when I was in second grade, black children integrated Central High School in Little Rock, Arkansas. We watched it on TV. All of us watched it. I don't mean Mama and Daddy and Rocky. I mean *all* the colored people in America watched it, together, with one set of eyes. We'd watch it in the morning, on the *Today* show on NBC, before we'd go to school; we'd watch it in the evening, on the news, with Edward R. Murrow on CBS. We'd watch the Special Bulletins at night, interrupting our TV shows.   18

The children were all well scrubbed and greased down, as we'd say. Hair short and closely cropped, parted, and oiled (the boys); "done" in a "permanent" and straightened, with turned-up bangs and curls (the girls). Starched shirts, white, and creased pants, shoes shining like a buck private's spit shine. Those Negroes were *clean*. The fact was, those   19 children trying to get the right to enter that school in Little Rock looked like black versions of models out of *Jack & Jill* magazine, to which my mama had subscribed for me so that I could see what children outside the valley were up to. "They hand-picked those children," Daddy would say. "No dummies, no nappy hair, heads not too kinky, lips not too thick, no disses and no dats." At seven, I was dismayed by his cynicism. It bothered me somehow that those children would have been chosen, rather than just having shown up or volunteered or been nearby in the neighborhood.

Daddy was jaundiced about the civil rights movement, and especially about the Reverend Dr. Martin Luther King, Jr. He'd say all of his names, to drag out his scorn. By the mid-sixties, we'd argue about King from sunup to sundown. Sometimes he'd just mention King to get a rise from me, to make a sagging evening more interesting, to see if I had *learned* anything real yet, to see how long I could think up counter arguments before getting so mad that my face would turn purple. I think he just liked the color purple on my face, liked producing it there. But he was not of two minds about those children in Little Rock.

The children would get off their school bus surrounded by soldiers from the National Guard and by a field of state police. They would stop at the steps of the bus and seem to take a very deep breath. Then the phalanx would start to move slowly along this gulley of sidewalk and rednecks that connected the steps of the school bus with the white wooden double doors of the school. All kinds of crackers would be lining that gulley, separated from the phalanx of children by rows of state police, who formed a barrier arm in arm. Cheerleaders from the all-white high school that was desperately trying to stay that way were dressed in those funny little pleated skirts, with a big red *C* for "Central" on their chest, and they'd wave their pom-poms and start to cheer: "Two, four, six, eight—We don't want to integrate!" And all those crackers and all those rednecks would join in that chant as if their lives depended on it. Deafening, it was: even on our twelve-inch TV, a three-inch speaker buried along the back of its left side.

Whatever tumult our small screen revealed, though, the dawn of the civil rights era could be no more than a spectator sport from our living room in Piedmont. It was almost like a war being fought overseas. And all things considered, white and colored Piedmont got along pretty well in those years, the fifties and early sixties. At least as long as colored people didn't try to sit down in the Cut-Rate or at the Rendezvous Bar, or eat pizza at Eddie's, or buy property, or move into the white neighborhoods, or dance with, date, or dilate upon white people. Not to mention try to get a job in the craft unions at the paper mill. Or have a drink at the white VFW, or join the white American Legion, or get loans at the bank, or just generally get out of line. Other than that, colored and white got on pretty well.

QUESTIONS FOR DISCUSSION

1   What ritual function did television play in the life of Gates's family?

2   What programs did Gates and his family watch on television and listen to on radio in the late 1950s and early 1960s? What images and sounds were he and his family "starved for"?

3   Why were Gates, his family, and the black community of Piedmont so obsessed by sports? Do you think the interest in sports among African-Americans is as intense today? Explain your response.

4   What did television teach Gates about white people? Do you think the images of white Americans in the shows he mentions were realistic or representative of that period?

5   What view of the civil rights movement did Gates construct after listening to his father? How was Gates's hometown in West Virginia both different from and similar to the world of the Deep South where the key events of the civil rights era took place?

IDEAS FOR WRITING

1   Write about a recent popular television show that has an all-minority cast. How realistic or stereotyped are the images of minority life presented in this show?

2   Psychiatrist Robert Coles has noted that the political views of young people are often formed through observation of their parents' responses to television news. Write an essay in which you reflect on how some of your own political views were formed through such responses and observations of historical events.

Gangsta Culture—Sexism, Misogyny: Who Will Take the Rap?

BELL HOOKS

*One of America's best-known black intellectuals, bell hooks
was born Gloria Watkins in rural Kentucky in 1952. She earned her
Ph.D. at Stanford University and has taught at Oberlin College, City
University of New York, and Yale University. Among her best-known
books are the autobiographical* Ain't I a Woman *(1981) and the essay
collections* Talking Back, Thinking Feminist, Thinking Black *(1989),*
Yearning: Race, Gender, and Cultural Politics *(1990),* Black Looks:
Race and Representation *(1992), and* Reel to Real: Race, Sex and
Class at the Movies *(1997). Her essays on popular and mass culture
focus on the ways that the marginalized state of black people is
portrayed through media images. She believes that mass culture,
even when produced by African-American directors or musicians,
reflects the stereotypes of the dominant culture. In the following
essay from her recent collection,* Outlaw Culture *(1994), she attempts
to explain the origins of the violent, mysogynistic viewpoint of
"gangsta rap" recordings.*

For the past several months, the white mainstream media has been   1
contacting me to hear my views on gangsta rap. Whether major television networks, or small independent radio shows, they seek me out
for the black and feminist take on the issue. After I have my say, I am
never called back, never invited to do the television shows, the radio
spots. I suspect they call me, confident that when we talk they will
hear the hardcore "feminist" trash of gangsta rap. When they encounter instead the hardcore feminist critique of white supremacist
capitalist patriarchy, they lose interest.

To the white-dominated mass media, the controversy over gangsta   2
rap makes great spectacle. Besides the exploitation of these issues to
attract audiences, a central motivation for highlighting gangsta rap
continues to be the sensationalist drama of demonizing black youth
culture in general and the contributions of young black men in particular. It's a contemporary remake of *Birth of a Nation*—only this time
we are encouraged to believe it is not just vulnerable white woman-
hood that risks destruction by black hands, but everyone. When I
counter this demonization of black males by insisting that gangsta rap
does not appear in a cultural vacuum, that it is not a product created
in isolation within a segregated black world but is rather expressive of
the cultural crossing, mixings, and engagement of black youth culture
with the values, attitudes, and concerns of the white majority, some
folks stop listening.

The sexist, misogynist, patriarchal ways of thinking and behaving   3
that are glorified in gangsta rap are a reflection of the prevailing values
in our society, values created and sustained by white supremacist
capitalist patriarchy. As the crudest and most brutal expression of sexism, misogynistic attitudes tend to be portrayed by the dominant culture as always an expression of male deviance. In reality, they are part
of a sexist continuum, necessary for the maintenance of patriarchal
social order. While patriarchy and sexism continue to be the political
and cultural norm in our society, the feminist movement has created
a climate where crude expressions of male domination are likely to be
called into question, especially if they are made by men in power. It is
useful to think of misogyny as a field that must be labored in and
maintained both to sustain patriarchy but also to nourish an antifeminist backlash. And what better group to labor on this "plantation"
than young black men?

To see gangsta rap as a reflection of dominant values in our culture   4
rather than as an aberrant pathological standpoint does not mean
that a rigorous feminist critique and interrogation of the sexism and
misogyny expressed in this music is not needed. Without a doubt
black males, young and old, must be held politically accountable for
their sexism. Yet this critique must always be contextualized or we risk
making it appear that the problems of misogyny, sexism, and all the
behaviors this thinking supports and condones, including rape, male
violence against women, are a black male thing. And this is what is happening. Young black males are forced to take the heat for encouraging
via their music the hatred of and violence against women that is a
central core of patriarchy.

Witness the recent piece by Brent Staples in the *New York Times,* en-   5
titled "The Politics of Gangster Rap: A Music Celebrating Murder and
Misogyny." Defining the turf, Staples writes, "For those who haven't
caught up, gangster rap is that wildly successful music in which all
women are 'bitches' and 'whores' and young men kill each other for
sport." No mention of white supremacist capitalist patriarchy in this
piece. Not a word about the cultural context that would need to exist
for young males to be socialized to think differently about gender. No
word about feminism. Staples unwittingly assumes that black males
are writing their lyrics off in the "jungle," faraway from the impact of
mainstream socialization and desire. At no point does he interrogate
why it is huge audiences, especially young white male consumers, are
so turned on by this music, by the misogyny and sexism, by the bru-
tality. Where is the anger and rage at females expressed in this music
coming from, the glorification of all acts of violence? These are the difficult questions that Staples feels no need to answer.

One cannot answer them honestly without placing accountability   6
on larger structures of domination (sexism, racism, class elitism) and
the individuals—often white, usually male, but not always—who are

hierarchically placed to maintain and perpetuate the values that up-
hold these exploitative and oppressive systems. That means taking a
critical look at the politics of hedonistic consumerism, the values
of the men and women who produce gangsta rap. It would mean
considering the seduction of young black males who find that they
can make more money producing lyrics that promote violence, sexism, misogyny than with any other content. How many disenfran-
chised black males would not surrender to expressing virulent forms
of sexism if they knew the rewards would be unprecedented material
power and fame?

More than anything, gangsta rap celebrates the world of the mate-   7
rial, the dog-eat-dog world where you do what you gotta do to make
it even if it means fucking over folks and taking them out. In this world
killing is necessary for survival. Significantly, the logic here is a crude
expression of the logic of white supremacist capitalist patriarchy. In
his new book *Sexy Dressing Etc.*, privileged white male law professor
Duncan Kennedy gives what he calls "a set of general characterizations
of U.S. culture," explaining that "it is individual (cowboys), material
(gangsters), and philistine." This general description of the mainstream culture would not lead us to place gangsta rap on the margins
of what this nation is about but at the center. Rather than seeing it as
a subversion or disruption of the norm, we would need to see it as an
embodiment of the norm.

That viewpoint was graphically highlighted in the film *Menace II*   8
Society, a drama not only of young black males killing for sport, but
which included scenes where mass audiences voyeuristically watched
and in many cases enjoyed the kill. Significantly, at one point in the
film we see that the young black males have learned their gangsta
values from watching movies and television and shows where white
male gangsters are center stage. The importance of this scene is how
it undermines any notion of "essentialist" blackness that would have
viewers believe that the gangsterism these young black males em-
braced emerged from some unique black cultural experience.

When I interviewed rap artist Ice Cube for *Spin* magazine recently,   9
he talked about the importance of respecting black women, of communication across gender. In our conversation, he spoke against male
violence against women, even as he lapsed into a justification for
antiwoman lyrics in rap by insisting on the madonna/whore split
where some females "carry" themselves in a manner that determines
how they will be treated. But when this interview came to press it was
sliced to ribbons. Once again it was a mass media set-up. Folks
(mostly white and male) had thought that if the hardcore feminist
talked with the hardened mack, sparks would fly; there would be a
knock-down, drag-out spectacle. When Brother Cube and myself
talked to each other with respect about the political, spiritual and
emotional self-determination of black people, it did not make good

copy. I do not know if his public relations people saw the piece in its entirety and were worried that it would be too soft an image, but clearly folks at the magazine did not get the darky spectacle they were looking for.

After this conversation, and after talking with other rappers and folks who listen to rap, it became clear that while black male sexism is real and a serious problem in our communities, some of the more misogynist stuff in black music was there to stir up controversy, to appeal to audiences. Nowhere is this more evident than in the image used with Snoop Doggy Dogg's record *Doggystyle.* A black male music and cultural critic called me from across the ocean to ask if I had checked this image out, sharing that for one of the first times in his music-buying life he felt he was seeing an image so offensive in its sexism and misogyny he did not want to take it home. That image— complete with doghouse, "Beware the Dog" sign, a naked black female head in the doghouse, her naked butt sticking out—was reproduced "uncritically" in the November 29, 1993, issue of *Time* magazine. The positive music review of this album written by Christopher John Farley titled "Gangsta Rap, Doggystyle" makes no mention of sexism and misogyny, or any reference to the cover. If a naked white female body had been inside the doghouse, presumably waiting to be fucked from behind, I wonder if *Time* would have reproduced an image of the cover along with their review. When I see the pornographic cartoon that graces the cover of *Doggystyle* I do not think simply about the sexism and misogyny of young black men, I think about the sexist and misogynist politics of the powerful white adult men and women (and folks of color) who helped produce and market this album.

In her book *Misogynies,* Joan Smith shares her sense that while most folks are willing to acknowledge unfair treatment of women, discrimination on the basis of gender, they are usually reluctant to admit that hatred of women is encouraged because it helps maintain the structure of male dominance. Smith suggests, "Misogyny wears many guises, reveals itself in different forms—which are dictated by class, wealth, education, race, religion, and other factors, but its chief characteristic is its pervasiveness." This point reverberated in my mind when I saw Jane Campion's widely acclaimed film *The Piano,* which I saw in the midst of the mass media's focus on sexism and misogyny in gangsta rap. I had been told by many friends in the art world that this was "an incredible film, a truly compelling love story." Their responses were echoed by numerous positive reviews. No one speaking about this film mentions misogyny and sexism or white supremacist capitalist patriarchy, which blithely ignores how the nineteenth-century world of the white invasion of New Zealand and the conquest of femininity are utterly romanticized in this film.

A racist white imagination assumes that most young black males, especially those who are poor, live in a self-created cultural vacuum, uninfluenced by mainstream cultural values. Yet it is the application of those values, largely learned through passive, uncritical consumption of the mass media, that is most revealed in gangsta rap. Brent Staples is willing to challenge the notion that "urban primitivism is romantic" when it suggests that black males become "real men" by displaying the will to do violence, yet he remains resolutely silent about that world of privileged white culture that has historically romanticized primitivism and eroticized male violence. Contemporary films like *Reservoir Dogs* and *Bad Lieutenant* celebrate urban primitivism. Many of the artistically less successful films create or exploit the cultural demand for graphic depictions of hardcore macks who are willing to kill for sport.

To take gangsta rap to task for its sexism and misogyny while accepting and perpetuating expressions of that ideology which reflect bourgeois standards (no rawness, no vulgarity) is not to call for a transformation of the culture of patriarchy. Ironically, many black male ministers who are themselves sexist and misogynist are leading the attacks against gangsta rap. Like the mainstream world that supports white supremacist capitalist patriarchy, they are the most concerned with advancing the cause of censorship by calling attention to the obscene portrayals of women. For them, rethinking and challenging sexism both in the dominant culture and in black life is not the issue.   13

Mainstream white culture is not at all concerned about black male sexism and misogyny, particularly when it is mainly unleashed against black women and children. It *is* concerned when young white consumers utilize black vernacular popular culture to disrupt bourgeois values. A young white boy expresses his rage at his mother by aping black male vernacular speech (a true story); young white males (and middle-class men of color) reject the constraints of bourgeois bondage and the call to be "civilized" by acts of aggression in their domestic households. These are the audiences who feel such a desperate need for gangsta rap. It is much easier to attack gangsta rap than to confront the culture that produces that need.   14

Gangsta rap is part of the antifeminist backlash that is the rage right now. When young black males labor in the plantations of misogyny and sexism to produce gangsta rap, white supremacist capitalist patriarchy approves the violence and materially rewards them. Far from being an expression of their "manhood," it is an expression of their own subjugation and humiliation by more powerful, less visible forces of patriarchal gangsterism. They give voice to the brutal, raw anger and rage against women that it is taboo for "civilized" adult men to speak. No wonder, then, that they have the task of tutoring the young, teaching them to eroticize and enjoy the brutal expressions of that rage (both language and acts) before they learn to cloak it in middle-class decorum or Robert Bly–style reclaimings of lost manhood. The tragedy   15 for young black males is that they are so easily duped by a vision of manhood that can only lead to their destruction.

Feminist critiques of the sexism and misogyny in gangsta rap, and in all aspects of popular culture, must continue to be bold and fierce. Black females must not allow ourselves to be duped into supporting shit that hurts us under the guise of standing beside our men. If black men are betraying us through acts of male violence, we save ourselves and the race by resisting. Yet our feminist critiques of black male sexism fail as meaningful political interventions if they seek to demonize black males, and do not recognize that our revolutionary work is to transform white supremacist capitalist patriarchy in the multiple areas of our lives where it is made manifest, whether in gangsta rap, the black church, or in the Clinton administration.

16

QUESTIONS FOR DISCUSSION

1   Why do the television and radio talk show people who call hooks about her views on "gangsta culture" lose interest when they hear her actual views? What does their disappointment reveal about the political attitudes reflected in talk show programming?

2   According to hooks, how and why are the attitudes toward violence and male domination of women in gangsta rap representative of mainstream white, capitalist, "patriarchal" culture? Do you agree?

3   How does hooks use examples from written texts, advertisements, interviews with gangsta rappers, as well as current films appealing to different audiences, to support her points? Is her use of evidence convincing?

4   Why does hooks criticize Brent Staples? Do her criticisms of his piece on rap seem justified and relevant to her larger argument?

5   Why does hooks think gangsta rap appeals to young white males?

IDEAS FOR WRITING

1   Write an essay based on your interviews with several young people from different ethnic backgrounds who enjoy gangsta rap. Why do they like this music? Are any of them influenced by the attitudes and language used by the rappers?

2   Write a response to hooks's essay from the perspective of one of the groups or individuals of whom she is critical, such as young white males, record producers, talk show hosts, or Brent Staples.

Hate Radio

PATRICIA J. WILLIAMS

A lawyer and college professor, Patricia J. Williams (b. 1951) is an outspoken defender of individuals and groups denied fundamental rights because of class, race, or gender. She received her B.A. from Wellesley College in 1972 and her J.D. in 1975 from Harvard Law School; since 1991 she has been a professor of law at Columbia University. Williams has been a contributor to a number of publications, including Contemporary Sociology, Ms., *the* Harvard Law Review, *the* New Yorker, *the* Washington Post, *and the* Nation, *where she writes a regular column, "Diary of a Mad Law Professor." She has also written two books,* The Alchemy of Race and Rights *(1991) and* The Rooster's Egg: On the Persistence of Prejudice *(1995). In the following essay, which appeared in* Ms. *in April 1994, Williams argues that "hate radio," the product of right-wing and sometimes racist commentators, is a dangerous media phenomenon that may harm race relations.*

Three years ago I stood at my sink, washing the dishes and listening to the radio. I was tuned to rock and roll so I could avoid thinking about the big news from the day before—George Bush had just nominated Clarence Thomas to replace Thurgood Marshall on the Supreme Court. I was squeezing a dot of lemon Joy into each of the wineglasses when I realized that two smoothly radio-cultured voices, a man's and a woman's, had replaced the music. 1

"I think it's a stroke of genius on the president's part," said the female voice. 2

"Yeah," said the male voice. "Then those blacks, those African Americans, those Negroes—hey 'Negro' is good enough for Thurgood Marshall—whatever, they can't make up their minds [what] they want to be called. I'm gonna call them Blafricans. Black Africans. Yeah, I like it. Blafricans. Then they can get all upset because now the president appointed a Blafrican." 3

"Yeah, well, that's the way those liberals think. It's just crazy." 4

"And then after they turn down his nomination the president can say he tried to please 'em, and then he can appoint someone with some intelligence." 5

Back then, this conversation seemed so horrendously unusual, so singularly hateful, that I picked up a pencil and wrote it down. I was certain that a firestorm of protest was going to engulf the station and purge those foul radio mouths with the good clean soap of social outrage. 6

I am so naive. When I finally turned on the radio and rolled my dial to where everyone else had been tuned while I was busy watching 7

Cosby reruns, it took me a while to understand that there's a firestorm all right, but not of protest. In the two and a half years since Thomas has assumed his post on the Supreme Court, the underlying assumptions of the conversation I heard as uniquely outrageous have become commonplace, popularly expressed, and louder in volume. I hear the style of that snide polemicism everywhere, among acquaintances, on the street, on television in toned-down versions. It is a crude demagoguery that makes me heartsick. I feel more and more surrounded by that point of view, the assumptions of being without intelligence, the coded epithets, the "Blafrican"-like stand-ins for "nigger," the mocking angry glee, the endless tirades filled with nonspecific, non-empirically based slurs against "these people" or "those minorities" or "feminazis" or "liberals" or "scumbags" or "pansies" or "jerks" or "sleazeballs" or "loonies" or "animals" or "foreigners."

At the same time I am not so naive as to suppose that this is something new. In clearheaded moments I realize I am not listening to the radio anymore, I am listening to a large segment of white America think aloud in even louder resurgent thoughts that have generations of historical precedent. It's as though the radio has split open like an egg, Morton Downey, Jr.'s clones and Joe McCarthy's ghost spilling out, broken yolks, a great collective of sometimes clever, sometimes small, but uniformly threatened brains—they have all come gushing out. Just as they were about to pass into oblivion, Jack Benny and his humble black sidekick Rochester get resurrected in the ungainly bodies of Howard Stern and his faithful black henchwoman, Robin Quivers. The culture of Amos and Andy has been revived and reassembled in Bob Grant's radio minstrelry and radio newcomer Daryl Gates's sanctimonious imprecations on behalf of decent white people. And in striking imitation of Jesse Helms's nearly forgotten days as a radio host, the far Right has found its undisputed king in the personage of Rush Limbaugh—a polished demagogue with a weekly radio audience of at least twenty million, a television show that vies for ratings with the likes of Jay Leno, a newsletter with a circulation of 380,000, and two best-selling books whose combined sales are closing in on six million copies.

From Churchill to Hitler to the old Soviet Union, it's clear that radio and television have the power to change the course of history, to proselytize, and to coalesce not merely the good and the noble, but the very worst in human nature as well. Likewise, when Orson Welles made his famous radio broadcast "witnessing" the landing of a spaceship full of hostile Martians, the United States ought to have learned a lesson about the power of radio to appeal to mass instincts and incite mass hysteria. Radio remains a peculiarly powerful medium even today, its visual emptiness in a world of six trillion flashing images allowing one of the few remaining playgrounds for the aural subconscious. Perhaps its power is attributable to our need for an oral tradition after all, some conveying of stories, feelings, myths of ancestors, epics of alienation, and the need to rejoin ancestral roots, even ignorant bigoted roots. Perhaps the visual quiescence of radio is related to the popularity of E-mail or electronic networking. Only the voice is made manifest, unmasking worlds that cannot—or dare not?—be seen. Just yet. Nostalgia crystallizing into a dangerous future. The preconscious voice erupting into the expressed, the prime time.

What comes out of the modern radio mouth could be the *Iliad,* the   10
Rubaiyat, the griot's song of our times. If indeed radio is a vessel for the American "Song of Songs," then what does it mean that a manic, adolescent Howard Stern is so popular among radio listeners, that Rush Limbaugh's wittily smooth sadism has gone the way of prime-time television, and that both vie for the number one slot on all the best-selling book lists? What to make of the stories being told by our modern radio evangelists and their tragic unloved chorus of callers? Is it really just a collapsing economy that spawns this drama of grown people sitting around scaring themselves to death with fantasies of black feminist Mexican able-bodied gay soldiers earning $100,000 a year on welfare who are so criminally depraved that Hillary Clinton or the antichrist-of-the-moment had no choice but to invite them onto the government payroll so they can run the country? The panicky exaggeration reminds me of a child's fear. . . . *And then, and then, a huge lion jumped out of the shadows and was about to gobble me up, and I can't ever sleep again for a whole week.*

As I spin the dial on my radio, I can't help thinking that this stuff   11
must be related to that most poignant of fiber-optic phenomena, phone sex. Aural Sex. Radio Racism with a touch of S & M. High-priest hosts with the power and run-amok ego to discipline listeners, to smack with the verbal back of the hand, to smash the button that shuts you up once and for all. "Idiot!" shouts New York City radio demagogue Bob Grant and then the sound of droning telephone emptiness, the voice of dissent dumped out some trap-door in aural space.

As I listened to a range of such programs what struck me as the most   12
unifying theme was not merely the specific intolerance on such hot topics as race and gender, but a much more general contempt for the world, a verbal stoning of anything different. It is like some unusually violent game of "Simon Says," this mockery and shouting down of callers, this roar of incantations, the insistence on agreement.

But, ah, if you *will* but only agree, what sweet and safe reward, what   13
soft enfolding by a stern and angry radio god. And as an added bonus, the invisible shield of an AM community, a family of fans who are Exactly Like You, to whom you can express, in anonymity, all the filthy stuff you imagine "them" doing to you. The comfort and relief of being able to ejaculate, to those who understand, about the dark imagined

excess overtaking, robbing, needing to be held down and taught a good lesson, needing to put it in its place before the ravenous demon enervates all that is true and good and pure in this life.

The audience for this genre of radio flagellation is mostly young, white, and male. Two thirds of Rush Limbaugh's audience is male. According to *Time* magazine, 75 percent of Howard Stern's listeners are white men. Most of the callers have spent their lives walling themselves off from any real experience with blacks, feminists, lesbians, or gays. In this regard, it is probably true, as former Secretary of Education William Bennett says, that Rush Limbaugh "tells his audience that what you believe inside, you can talk about in the marketplace." Unfortunately, what's "inside" is then mistaken for what's outside, treated as empirical and political reality. The *National Review* extols Limbaugh's conservative leadership as no less than that of Ronald Reagan, and the Republican party provides Limbaugh with books to discuss, stories, angles, and public support. "People were afraid of censure by gay activists, feminists, environmentalists—now they are not because Rush takes them on," says Bennett.   14

U.S. history has been marked by cycles in which brands of this or that hatred come into fashion and go out, are unleashed and then restrained. If racism, homophobia, jingoism, and woman-hating have been features of national life in pretty much all of modern history, it rather begs the question to spend a lot of time wondering if right-wing radio is a symptom or a cause. For at least four hundred years, prevailing attitudes in the West have considered African Americans less intelligent. Recent statistics show that 53 percent of people in the U.S. agree that blacks and Latinos are less intelligent than whites, and a majority believe that blacks are lazy, violent, welfare-dependent, and unpatriotic.   15

I think that what has made life more or less tolerable for "out" groups have been those moments in history when those "inside" feelings were relatively restrained. In fact, if I could believe that right-wing radio were only about idiosyncratic, singular, rough-hewn individuals thinking those inside thoughts, I'd be much more inclined to agree with Columbia University media expert Everette Dennis, who says that Stern's and Limbaugh's popularity represents the "triumph of the individual" or with *Time* magazine's bottom line that "the fact that either is seriously considered a threat . . . is more worrisome than Stern or Limbaugh will ever be." If what I were hearing had even a tad more to do with real oppressions, with real white *and* black levels of joblessness and homelessness, or with the real problems of real white men, then I wouldn't have bothered to slog my way through hours of Howard Stern's miserable obsessions.   16

Yet at the heart of my anxiety is the worry that Stern, Limbaugh, Grant et al. represent the very antithesis of individualism's triumph. As the *National Review* said of Limbaugh's ascent, "It was a feat not   17 only of the loudest voice but also of a keen political brain to round up, as Rush did, the media herd and drive them into the conservative corral." When asked about his political aspirations, Bob Grant gloated to the *Washington Post,* "I think I would make rather a good dictator."

The polemics of right-wing radio are putting nothing less than hate   18
onto the airwaves, into the marketplace, electing it to office, teaching it in schools, and exalting it as freedom. What worries me is the increasing-to-constant commerce of retribution, control, and lashing out, fed not by fact but fantasy. What worries me is the reemergence, more powerfully than at any time since the institution of Jim Crow, of a socio-centered self that excludes "the likes of," well, me for example, from the civic circle, and that would rob me of my worth and claim and identity as a citizen. As the *Economist* rightly observes, "Mr. Limbaugh takes a mass market—white, mainly male, middle-class, ordinary America—and talks to it as an endangered minority."

I worry about this identity whose external reference is a set of   19
beliefs, ethics, and practices that excludes, restricts, and acts in the world on me, or mine, as the perceived if not real enemy. I am acutely aware of losing *my* mythic individualism to the surface shapes of my mythic group fearsomeness as black, as female, as left wing. "I" merge not fluidly but irretrievably into a category of "them." I become a suspect self, a moving target of loathsome properties, not merely different but dangerous. And that worries me a lot.

What happens in my life with all this translated license, this per-   20
mission to be uncivil? What happens to the social space that was supposedly at the sweet mountaintop of the civil rights movement's trail? Can I get a seat on the bus without having to be reminded that I *should* be standing? Did the civil rights movement guarantee us nothing more than to use public accommodations while surrounded by raving lunatic bigots? "They didn't beat this idiot [Rodney King] enough," says Howard Stern.

Not long ago I had the misfortune to hail a taxicab in which the   21
driver was listening to Howard Stern undress some woman. After some blocks, I had to get out. I was, frankly, afraid to ask the driver to turn it off—not because I was afraid of "censoring" him, which seems to be the only thing people will talk about anymore, but because the driver was stripping me too, as he leered through the rearview mirror. "Something the matter?" he demanded, as I asked him to pull over and let me out well short of my destination. (I'll spare you the full story of what happened from there—trying to get another cab, as the cabbies stopped for all the white businessmen who so much as scratched their heads near the curb; a nice young white man, seeing my plight, giving me his cab, having to thank him, he hero, me saved-but-humiliated, cabdriver pissed and surly. I fight my way to my destination, finally arriving in bad mood, militant black woman, cranky femi-nazi.)

When Yeltsin blared rock music at his opponents holed up in the   22
parliament building in Moscow, in imitation of the U.S. Marines trying
to torture Manuel Noriega in Panama, all I could think of was that it
must be like being trapped in a crowded subway car when all the
portable stereos are tuned to Bob Grant or Howard Stern. With Howard
Stern's voice a tinny, screeching backdrop, with all the faces growing
dreamily mean as though some soporifically evil hallucinogen were
gushing into their bloodstreams, I'd start begging to surrender.

Surrender to what? Surrender to the laissez-faire resegregation that   23
is the metaphoric significance of the hundreds of "Rush rooms" that
have cropped up in restaurants around the country; rooms broadcasting Limbaugh's words, rooms for your listening pleasure, rooms
where bigots can capture the purity of a Rush-only lunch counter,
rooms where all those unpleasant others just "choose" not to eat? Surrender to the naughty luxury of a room in which a Ku Klux Klan meet-
ing could take place in orderly, First Amendment fashion? Everyone's
"free" to come in (and a few of you outsiders do), but mostly the
undesirable nonconformists are gently repulsed away. It's a high-tech
world of enhanced choice. Whites choose mostly to sit in the Rush
room. Feminists, blacks, lesbians, and gays "choose" to sit elsewhere.
No need to buy black votes, you just pay them not to vote; no need to
insist on white-only schools, you just sell the desirability of black-only
schools. Just sit back and watch it work, like those invisible shock
shields that keep dogs cowering in their own backyards.

How real is the driving perception behind all the Sturm and Drang   24
of this genre of radio-harangue—the perception that white men are
an oppressed minority, with no power and no opportunity in the land
that they made great? While it is true that power and opportunity are
shrinking for all but the very wealthy in this country (and would that
Limbaugh would take that issue on), the fact remains that white men
are still this country's most privileged citizens and market actors. To
give just a small example, according to the *Wall Street Journal,* blacks
were the only racial group to suffer a net job loss during the 1990–91
economic downturn at the companies reporting to the Equal Employment Opportunity Commission. Whites, Latinos, and Asians, mean-
while, gained thousands of jobs. While whites gained 71,144 jobs at
these companies, Latinos gained 60,040, Asians gained 55,104, and
blacks lost 59,479. If every black were hired in the United States to-
morrow, the numbers would not be sufficient to account for white
men's expanding balloon of fear that they have been specifically dis-
possessed by African Americans.

Given deep patterns of social segregation and general ignorance of   25
history, particularly racial history, media remain the principal source
of most Americans' knowledge of each other. Media can provoke violence or induce passivity. In San Francisco, for example, a radio show

on KMEL called "Street Soldiers" has taken this power as a responsibility with great consequence: "Unquestionably," writes Ken Auletta in the *New Yorker,* "the show has helped avert violence. When a Samoan teenager was slain, apparently by Filipino gang members, in a drive-by shooting, the phones lit up with calls from Samoans wanting to tell [the hosts] they would not rest until they had exacted revenge. Threats filled the air for a couple of weeks. Then the dead Samoan's father called in, and, in a poignant exchange, the father said he couldn't tolerate the thought of more young men senselessly slaughtered. There would be no retaliation, he vowed. "And there was none." In contrast, we must wonder at the phenomenon of the very powerful leadership of the Republican party, from Ronald Reagan to Robert Dole to William Bennett, giving advice, counsel, and friendship to Rush Limbaugh's passionate divisiveness.

The outright denial of the material crisis at every level of U.S. society, most urgently in black inner-city neighborhoods but facing us all, is a kind of political circus, dissembling as it feeds the frustrations of the moment. We as a nation can no longer afford to deal with such crises by *imagining* an excess of bodies, of babies, of job-stealers, of welfare mothers, of overreaching immigrants, of too-powerful (Jewish, in whispers) liberal Hollywood, of lesbians and gays, of gang members ("gangsters" remain white, and no matter what the atrocity, less vilified than "gang members," who are black), of Arab terrorists, and uppity women. The reality of our social poverty far exceeds these scapegoats. This right-wing backlash resembles, in form if not substance, phenomena like anti-Semitism in Poland: there aren't but a handful of Jews left in that whole country, but the giant balloon of heated anti-Semitism flourishes apace, Jews blamed for the world's evils.

26

The overwhelming response to right-wing excesses in the United States has been to seek an odd sort of comfort in the fact that the First Amendment is working so well that you can't suppress this sort of thing. Look what's happened in Eastern Europe. Granted. So let's not talk about censorship or the First Amendment for the next ten minutes. But in Western Europe, where fascism is rising at an appalling rate, suppression is hardly the problem. In Eastern and Western Europe as well as the United States, we must begin to think just a little bit about the fiercely coalescing power of media to spark mistrust, to fan it into forest fires of fear and revenge. We must begin to think about the levels of national and social complacence in the face of such resolute ignorance. We must ask ourselves what the expected result is, not of censorship or suppression, but of so much encouragement, so much support, so much investment in the fashionability of hate. What future is it that we are designing with the devotion of such tremendous resources to the disgraceful propaganda of bigotry?

27

QUESTIONS FOR DISCUSSION

1 How does the domestic scene with which Williams begins her essay contrast with what she hears on the radio?

2 What does Williams mean by the simile "the radio has split open like an egg"? What is coming out of the egg?

3 What underlying fear does racist talk radio prey on? What kind of generalized contempt do such programs express, according to Williams? What reward do the programs bring their listeners?

4 Despite the emphasis in the conservative belief system on individuality, how does right-wing talk radio represent "the very antithesis of individualism's triumph"?

5 What power, according to Williams, do the right-wing talk radio programs have to change racial attitudes? What examples does she give to support her arguments about the power and the dangers of this medium?

IDEAS FOR WRITING

1 Although freedom of speech is protected by the First Amendment, some people believe that censorship of extremist hate speech in media such as radio or the Internet should be an option in our society. Write an essay in which you take a position on the issue of censorship of hate speech.

2 In paragraph 25, Williams introduces a positive note through her example of the San Francisco radio show *Street Soldiers*. Write an essay in which you examine other examples of radio's being used as a positive social force for overcoming hatred and violence.

student essay

Not in My Living Room

LAURA CHYU

*Laura Chyu was born and grew up in Cupertino, California,
a suburb with a large Asian population. Her parents taught her
about Chinese traditions, while she learned about American culture
from school and friends. Chyu hopes to attend medical school after
graduating from Stanford University and specialize in psychiatry and
social evolution, particularly the evolutionary design of the body in
relation to food and eating habits. The following essay is a personal
response to "The Living Room" by Henry Louis Gates, Jr.*

Henry Louis Gates writes in his essay "The Living Room" of how he   1
observed images and stereotypes, discovered white culture, took pride
in the accomplishments of African-American athletes, and watched
the unfolding of the civil rights movement—all on TV. Gates's refer-
ences to shows remembered from his childhood demonstrate the
crucial impact of African-American images on television on his own
developing knowledge of the world around him. In contrast to the
experience of Gates and other African Americans, I did not find, growing up as an Asian American, that television played an important role
in the development of my cultural identity.

While African Americans held conspicuous roles in the television   2
industry even when Gates was a child, Asians are still struggling to
emerge as a visible race and culture in the media. Growing up and ab-
sorbing the media surrounding me, I assimilated information mostly
about white America, mainly because there were practically no Asian
characters in the media to relate to. It was not through the media that
I discovered my culture and identity, but rather through real-life interactions with my family, friends, and community. The absence of Asian
faces in the media continues to disturb me. To this day, Asians and
Asian Americans are still an almost invisible group in the media. As
Gish Jen states in her essay "Challenging the Asian Illusion," "For a
very long time, when people talked about race, they talked about
black America and white America. Where did that put Asian Americans? . . . We were somehow borderline; we did not quite belong."

Perhaps because Asian Americans did not experience as much of   3
the overtly destructive discrimination that other groups in America
have encountered, they have not been perceived in dramatic enough
terms to be visible in the mass media. Consequently, the few portrayals
of Asians and Asian Americans in mainstream media have been and
continue to be fleeting, underdeveloped, and stereotypical. Today we

may not see grotesquely distorted images of Asians such as the awkward and ugly landlord in *Breakfast at Tiffany's* or the evil Fu Manchu, but we still see Asians playing mostly limited, secondary roles.

The most popular Asian characters in movies and television share   4
common characteristics. For example, Bruce Lee and Jackie Chan became popular mainly because they possessed amazing and impressive martial arts skills. It seems as if the public needs something more than mere representation of a normal Asian character to capture their attention; it is almost expected for an Asian male star to be able to perform flashy kicks and punches if he is to appear on screen. Popular movies and television shows that incorporate Asian themes and characters are almost always inextricably related to martial arts. *Karate Kid, The Vanishing Son, Mortal Kombat,* and the *Legend of Kung Fu* are all examples of this relationship.

Gates related to *Amos and Andy* as a world that "was all colored,   5
just like ours"; it was a world that was somewhat realistic and relevant to the individuals that watched it, most of whom lived in segregated communities. In contrast, the settings created in martial arts–related shows and movies are not at all realistic to the average Asian American. These extravagant maneuvers and dramatic situations may be entertaining to watch, but they are not things that Asian Americans can relate to in everyday life.

Although Asian Americans are encountered more frequently in the   6
media today, many of the newer roles fail to reflect any substantial response to or understanding of Asian culture. The lack of differentiation of Asian-American characters from other cast members in some recent shows suggests that they were given the roles simply to convey a sense of diversity in the cast. For instance, the short-lived television series *The Single Guy* featured talented Asian-American actress Ming-na Wen as the predictable wife of one of the main characters, a young white male. In dress, mannerisms, speech, and appearance, Wen appeared very "all-American"; with no Asian friends or family on the show, she carried the image of the "assimilated" Asian to an extreme degree. Some may perceive this portrayal as positive because it seemingly defies the typical Asian stereotype. Nevertheless, Wen's character conveyed clichéd Asian characteristics of diligence, meticulousness, and efficiency, qualities given more emphasis through the show's contrast between Wen's fussiness and the disorganized, eccentric personality of her husband on the show. This Americanized, "safe" Asian image is reminiscent of the children that Gates describes entering the school in Little Rock as the "black version of models out of *Jack & Jill* magazine." Because of the potentially dangerous power to convey powerful, distorted images, novelist Gish Jen believes the media essentially colonize Asians and other "invisible" minorities that lack the power to create their own public depictions, thus constructing a "form onto which white writers have freely projected their fears and desires" (Jen 470).

Television and film portrayals of Asians have improved somewhat   7
over the past decade. Comedian and actress Margaret Cho has gained
popularity for her unconventional humor, while *Nash Bridges* has recently introduced a female Asian-American detective who challenges
traditional Asian stereotypes. *Star Trek* also has incorporated Asian
characters without the tendency to stereotype. In the most recent *Star
Trek* program, *Voyager,* Gareth Wang plays Ensign Harry Kim, a valu-
able member of the crew who contributes a great deal to the show's
plot and dynamics through intelligence and engaging personality.

Despite a few breakthroughs, the fact remains that it is still rare to   8
see Asian Americans in movies, television shows, or commercials,
and it will take considerably more time until Asian Americans are
fully integrated and visible in American media. Since there is an obvious need for meaningful role models and accurate media portrayals, more Asian Americans need to seek careers in media-related
fields where they currently are underrepresented, including acting,
modeling, filmmaking, and broadcasting. Although authors such as
Maxine Hong Kingston and Amy Tan and filmmakers such as Wayne
Wang and John Woo have turned their creative powers to humanizing
the Asian-American image, until the media present images and per-
formers that reflect the complexity and humanity of the Asian race
and culture, Asian Americans will continue to rely primarily on interactions with family, friends, and environment to discover their background. While a complete representation of the complexity of the
Asian culture may not be completely attainable, there is still much
room for progress and improvement.

QUESTIONS FOR DISCUSSION

1   What are the primary differences and causes of the differences
    that Chyu notices between the presentation of African-Americans
    and Asian Americans in television and film? Can you think of
    other distinctions and causes?

2   Although Chyu says that she was not influenced by the media be-
    cause she did not see Asians portrayed there, does she seem to
    have been affected by the "invisibility" of Asians in the media?
    What impact, positive or negative, might this lack of portrayal
    have on a group's self-esteem?

3   What critical point does Chyu make through her example of the
    Asian-American character in *The Single Guy?* What is objection-
    able about this character, despite her positive qualities?

4   What is meant by Gish Jen's statement about the "invisible" mi-
    nority as a "form onto which white writers have freely projected
    their fears and desires"? In what sense might such a minority be
    said to be "colonized"?

5   Chyu can find only a few examples of acceptable portrayals of Asian Americans in the media. What does she like about ex- amples she uses? Are her criteria for a "good" portrayal clear?

IDEAS FOR WRITING

1   Write an evaluation of a recent film or television portrayal of an Asian-American character in a central or secondary role. Using some of Chyu's criticisms and adding your own ideas, did you find the presentation interesting and realistic or stereotypical? Why?

2   Write an essay giving an idea for an interesting and timely dra- matic or comedy series featuring Asian Americans (or members of another underrepresented minority group) as central charac- ters. What barriers to success might such a show encounter? Why are so few such shows produced?

Reality Reconfigured: Reading the New Electronic Media

On Reading a Video Text

ROBERT SCHOLES

A professor at Brown University in English and comparative literature since 1970, Robert Scholes (b. 1929) has advocated new modes of expression in modern literature and urged alternative methods of critical response to imaginative texts in his innovative textbooks and critical studies such as Structuralism in Literature *(1974),* Fabulation and Metafiction *(1979), and* Semiotics and Interpretation *(1982). Currently Scholes is associated with the Department of Modern Culture and Media at Brown, where he is working on producing on-line editions of avant-garde magazines and hypertextual essays while overseeing the development of the Pacesetter English course for high school students, which includes reading and analysis of traditional literature as well as films and multimedia. The following essay from Scholes's* The Protocols of Reading *(1989) explores techniques for "reading" videos and advertisements as texts.*

The moments of surrender proposed to us by video texts come in many forms, but all involve a complex dynamic of power and pleasure. We are, for instance, offered a kind of power through the enhancement of our vision. Close-ups position us where we could never stand. Slow motion allows us an extraordinary penetration into the mechanics of movement, and, combined with music, lends a balletic grace to ordinary forms of locomotion. Filters and other devices cause us to see the world through jaundiced or rose-colored optics, coloring events with emotion more effectively than verbal pathetic fallacy and less obtrusively. These derangements of normal visual processing can be seen as either constraints or extensions of visual power—that is, as power over the viewer or as extensions of the viewer's own optical power, or both. Either way they offer us what is perhaps the greatest single virtue of art: change from the normal, a defense against the ever-present threat of boredom. Video texts, like all except the most utilitarian forms of textuality, are constructed upon a base of boredom, from which they promise us relief. 1

Visual fascination—and I have mentioned only a few of its obvious forms—is just one of the matrices of power and pleasure that are organized by video texts. Others include narrativity and what I should like to call, at least tentatively, cultural reinforcement. By narrativity, of course, I mean the pleasures and powers associated with the reception of stories presented in video texts. By cultural reinforcement, I mean the process through which video texts confirm viewers in their ideological positions and reassure them as to their membership in a collective cultural body. This function, which operates in the ethical-political realm, is an extremely important element of video textuality 2 and, indeed, an extremely important dimension of all the mass media. This is a function performed throughout much of human history by literature and the other arts, but now, as the arts have become more estranged from their own culture and even opposed to it, the mass media have come to perform this role. What the epic poem did for ancient cultures, the romance for feudalism, and the novel for bourgeois society, the media—and especially television—now do for the commodified, bureaucratized world that is our present environment.

It is time, now, to look at these processes as they operate in some specific texts. Let us begin with a well-known Budweiser commercial, which tells—most frequently in a format of twenty-eight seconds, though a longer version also exists—the life story of a black man pursuing a career as a baseball umpire. In this brief period of time, we are given enough information to construct an entire life story—provided we have the cultural knowledge upon which this construction depends. The story we construct is that of a young man from the provinces, who gets his "big break," his chance to make it in the big city, to rise to the top of his profession. We see him working hard in the small-time, small-town atmosphere of the minor leagues, where the pace of events is slower and more relaxed than it is "at the top." He gets his chance for success—the voice-over narrator says, "In the minors you got to make all the calls, and then one day you *get* the call"—after which we see him face his first real test. He must call an important and "close" play correctly and then withstand the pressure of dispute, neither giving ground by changing his mind (which would be fatal) nor reacting too vigorously to the challenge of his call by an offended manager. His passing of this test and being accepted is presented through a later scene in a bar, in which the manager who had staged the protest "toasts" the umpire with a bottle of Budweiser beer, with a chorus in the background singing, "You keep America working. This Bud's for you." From this scene we conclude that the ump has now "made it" and will live happily ever after. From a few scenes, then, aided by the voice-over narration and a music track, we construct an entire life. How do we do this? We draw upon a storehouse of cultural information that extends from fairy tales and other basic narrative structures to knowledge about the game and business of baseball.

In processing a narrative text we actually construct the story, bringing a vast repertory of cultural knowledge to bear upon the text that we are contemplating. Our pleasure in the narrative is to some extent a constructive pleasure, based upon the sense of accomplishment we achieve by successfully completing this task. By "getting" the story, we prove our competence and demonstrate our membership in a cultural community. And what is the story that we "get"? It is the myth of America itself, of the racial melting pot, of upward mobility, of justice done without fear or favor. The corporate structure of baseball, with minor leagues offering a path for the talented to the celebrity and financial rewards of the majors, embodies values that we all possess, we Americans, as one of the deepest parts of our cultural heritage or ideology. It is, of course, on the playing field that talent triumphs most easily over racial or social barriers. Every year in baseball new faces arrive. Young men, having proved themselves in the minors, get their chance to perform at the highest level. Yale graduates and high-school dropouts who speak little or no English are judged equally by how well they hit, run, throw, and react to game situations. If baseball is still the national pastime, it is because in it our cherished myths materialize—or appear to materialize.

The commercial we are considering is especially interesting because it shows us a black man competing not with his body but with his mind, his judgment and his emotions, in a cruelly testing public arena. Americans who attend to sports are aware that black athletes are just beginning to find acceptance at certain "leadership" positions, such as quarterback in professional football, and that there is still an active scandal over the slender representation of blacks at baseball's managerial and corporate levels. The case of the black umpire reminds viewers of these problems, even as it suggests that here, too, talent will finally prevail. The system works, America works. We can take pride in this. The narrative reduces its story to the absolutely bare essentials, making a career turn, or seem to turn, on a single decision. The ump must make a close call, which will be fiercely contested by a manager who is deliberately testing him. This is a story of initiation, in that respect, an ordeal that the ump must meet successfully. The text ensures that we know this is a test, by showing us the manager plotting in his dugout, and it gives us a manager with one of those baseball faces (Irish? German?) that have the history of the game written on them. This is not just partisan versus impartial judge, it is old man against youth and white against black. We root for the umpire because we want the system to work—not just baseball but the whole thing: America. For the story to work, of course, the ump must make the right call, and we must know it to be right. Here, the close-up and slow motion come into play—just as they would in a real instant replay—to let us see both how close the call is and that the umpire has indeed made the right call. The runner is out. The manager's charge from the dugout is classic baseball protest, and the ump's self-control and slow walk away from the angry manager are gestures in a ritual we all know. That's right, we think, that's the way it's done. We know these moves the way the contemporaries of Aeschylus and Sophocles knew the myths upon which the Greek tragedies were based. Baseball is already a ritual, and a ritual we partake of mostly through the medium of television. The commercial has only to organize these images in a certain way to create a powerful narrative.

At the bar after the game, we are off stage, outside that ritual of baseball, but we are still in the world of myth. The manager salutes the ump with his tilted bottle of beer; the old man acknowledges that youth has passed its test. The sword on the shoulder of knighthood, the laying on of hands, the tilted Bud—all these are ritual gestures in the same narrative structure of initiation. To the extent that we have wanted this to happen we are gratified by this closing scene of the narrative text, and many things, as I have suggested, conspire to make us want this ending. We are dealing with an archetypal narrative that has been adjusted for maximum effect within a particular political and social context, and all this has been deployed with a technical skill in casting, directing, acting, photographing, and editing that is of a high order. It is very hard to resist the pleasure of this text, and we cannot accept the pleasure without, for the bewildering minute at least, also accepting the ideology that is so richly and closely entangled with the story that we construct from the video text. To accept the pleasure of this text is to believe that America works; and this is a comforting belief, itself a pleasure of an even higher order—for as long as we can maintain it. Does the text also sell Budweiser? This is something only market research (if you believe it) can tell. But it surely sells the American way first and then seeks to sell its brand of beer by establishing a metonymic connection between the product and the nation: a national beer for the national pastime.

An audience that can understand this commercial, successfully constructing the ump's story from the scenes represented in the text and the comments of the narrative voice, is an audience that understands narrative structure and has a significant amount of cultural knowledge as well, including both data (how baseball leagues are organized, for instance, and how the game is played) and myth (what constitutes success, for example, and what initiation is). At a time when critics such as William Bennett and E. D. Hirsch are bewailing our ignorance of culture, it is important to realize that many Americans are not without culture; they simply have a different culture from that of Bennett and Hirsch. What they really lack, for the most part, is any way of analyzing and criticizing the power of a text like the Budweiser commercial—not its power to sell beer, which is easily resisted, especially once you have tasted better beer—but its power to sell America. For the sort of analysis that I am suggesting, it is necessary to recover (as Eliot says) from the surrender to this text, and it is also necessary to have the tools of ideological criticism. Recovery, in fact, may depend upon critical analysis, which is why the analysis of video texts needs to be taught in all our schools.   7

. . . We would do well to . . . consider the necessity of ideological criticism. One dimension of the conservative agenda for this country has been conspicuously anticritical. The proposals of William Bennett and E. D. Hirsch, for instance, different as they are in certain respects, are both recipes for the indoctrination of young people in certain cultural myths. The great books of past ages, in the eyes of Bennett,   8

Hirsch, and Allan Bloom, are to be mythologized, turned into frozen monuments of Greatness in which our "cultural heritage" is embodied. This is precisely what Bloom does to Plato, for instance, turning the dialectical search for truth into a fixed recipe for "greatness of soul." The irony of this is that Plato can only die in this process. Plato's work can better be kept alive in our time by such irreverent critiques as that of Jacques Derrida, who takes Plato seriously as an opponent, which is to say, takes him dialectically. In this age of massive manipulation and disinformation, criticism is the only way we have of taking something seriously. The greatest patriots in our time will be those who explore our ideology critically, with particular attention to the gaps between mythology and practice. Above all, we must start with our most beloved icons, not the ones we profess allegiance to, but those that really have the power to move and shake us.

QUESTIONS FOR DISCUSSION

1   According to Scholes, how does watching video texts evoke complex feelings of power and pleasure?

2   According to Scholes, why does viewing the narratives presented by video create a sense of "cultural reinforcement"?

3   How does the analysis of the Budweiser commercial about an African-American man's career as a baseball umpire help to illustrate Scholes's point about the feelings of pleasure, power, and cultural reinforcement provided by video texts? How does this commercial relate "the myth of America itself"?

4   What is Scholes's response to the complaints of Allan Bloom, E. D. Hirsch, and William Bennett about Americans' lack of cultural knowledge? Do you agree with him here?

5   According to Scholes, what is "ideological criticism," and why is it that Americans have difficulty performing such criticism? Do you agree?

IDEAS FOR WRITING

1   Employing the analytical and critical approach Scholes used in his criticism of the Budweiser commercial, write an "ideological criticism" of a brief video text: a TV commercial, a rock video, or an episode of a sitcom that embodies an aspect of the modern-day "myth of America."

2   Scholes's approach to a critical "reading" of contemporary mass culture is quite different from that of Allan Bloom and E. D. Hirsch, who favor encouraging the reading of classics from the Western canon. Whose approach do you prefer, if either? Write an essay that states and defends your position.

The Tales They Tell in Cyber-Space

JON KATZ

Jon Katz (b. 1938) has had a long writing career as a journalist, playwright, and novelist. After attending Antioch College, City College of New York, and the New School for Social Research, Katz worked for twelve years in textile design. In 1976 he published a collection of documents on the history of gay life in the United States, A Gay History. *His reviews and critical articles on the media have appeared in the* Nation, Rolling Stone, *the* Columbia Journalism Review, *and* New York. *His most recent books are* Virtuous Reality: How America Surrendered Discussion of Moral Values to Opportunists, Nitwits, and Blockheads Like William Bennett *(1997) and* Media Rants: Post-politics in the Digital Nation *(1997). In the following selection, which appeared originally in the* New York Times *in 1994, Katz examines the kind of in-depth exchanges that sometimes occur in on-line discussion groups.*

> My daughter has cancer. As some of you know, she is 8. In all the world I never conceived of all the sorrow I would feel at learning this, all the horror at watching her suffer so stoically through test after test. There is not a lot of hope, just a lot of medicine. We are preparing ourselves for the worst, which her doctor has hinted is what we should expect. I've decided to journal you every day, those of you who can bear to read it. Feel free to answer, to offer sympathy, encouragement or whatever else you're feeling. Please feel free to check me if I am too sorry for myself or for her.
>
> We are, as J— herself said, all going to die, and maybe this will help me to bear it. I do not know how to tell her grandparents, or even our friends, for she is much loved, inside and out of the house.
>
> We can start here. She asked me this morning, "Dad, does it get better? It does, doesn't it?" My mouth moved up and down, but nothing came out of it. I could sure use some words.
>
> —Excerpted with permission from
> the computer bulletin board
> Compuserve

With a cautionary nod toward technology's drum-beating prophets, we offer an understatement: our creative lives have changed. As happened when the printing press, the telephone and television were invented, stories and the means by which we tell them will never be the same, not for the people who tell them or for those who take them in. All over the world, the gatekeepers are disintegrating as the few who always decided what stories the rest of us would hear are yielding to the millions telling their stories directly to one another.

Of the thousands of potential books, magazine articles, films or television series, only a tiny fraction ever make it through all the checkpoints. Producers select a dozen or so stories for broadcast each night; book editors say no many more times than yes. As the career-obsessed producer in "The Player" said: "We get 50,000 pitches a year for movies. We pick 12."

But increasingly, technology is breaking down the notion of few-   3
to-many communications. Some communicators will always be more powerful than others, but the big idea behind cyber-tales is that for the first time the many are talking to the many. Every day, those who can afford the computer equipment and the telephone bills can be their own producers, agents, editors and audiences. Their stories are becoming more and more idiosyncratic, interactive and individualistic, told in different forums to diverse audiences in different ways.

The roads on which these stories move are the computer bulletin   4
board systems. There are more than 33,000 of them in the United States, and more than 11 million Americans are using them. Above them all hovers the most enormous information entity in history, Internet, the mystic global computer network. It carries more stories, messages and information each day than otherwise moves around the world in months.

"Finding the WELL was like discovering a cozy little world that had   5
been flourishing without me, hidden within the walls of my house; an entire cast of characters welcomed me to the troupe with great merriment a soon as I found the secret door," writes Howard Rheingold in "The Virtual Community: Homesteading on the Electronic Frontier." "Like others who fell into the WELL, I soon discovered that I was audience, performer and scriptwriter, along with my companions, in an ongoing improvisation."

The WELL Mr. Rheingold fell into—the Whole Earth 'Lectronic   6
Link, based north of San Francisco—was one of the first and most significant computer bulletin board systems. Small even by cyber-standards (it has 8,000 members, compared with America On Line's 450,000), the WELL is the creative and spiritual home of the computer culture, a combination think tank, unofficial legislature, conference center, production company, forum and village green. Unlike such larger systems as Prodigy and Compuserve, the WELL sells nothing but the ideas, expertise, curiosity and sometimes the friendship of its members—and their stories, of an astonishing power and range.

The WELL, like its electronic sisters around the planet, is helping to   7
redefine what a story is and giving us greater control over the creation and distribution of our own narratives than we have ever had. Ever more quickly and dramatically, the technology is liberating our individual and collective creative visions.

I live on the border between the old and the new cultures, be-   8
tween one kind of story and another. As a former editor, I was one of the few whose hands were on the machinery that transmits stories to

the many. When I bought a modem last year, I passed through the common and predictable stages of panic, frustration, confusion, shock and excitement. Although guided at each step by countless electronic helping hands, I felt incompetent.

But it was clear from the beginning—when I first logged on to the   9
WELL, typed "Help!" and was flooded with messages of welcome— that I had transported myself to a place I had read about but had not even begun to imagine.

Once I had mastered the machinery, I found myself adrift in a sea   10
of stories, more than I could absorb or measure. They washed over me as the people around me passed back and forth not only literal news of the world, but also debate and information via dozens of growing and evolving electronic conferences—on parenting, poetry, AIDS, sex, religion, aging, virtual reality, feminism, music, psychology. Everyone was telling stories; in fact, everyone was redefining the very form and function of a story. At least that was one way of looking at it.

A story was no longer something acquired and distributed by an   11
editor, network or publisher. A story was an experience, anecdote, musing or argument that could be tossed off into space for electronic pilgrims to digest, applaud or ignore. It was never clear where it would land or what might come back as a result. Stories almost always brought a response—sympathy, another story, criticism, laughter. In this sense, they became interactive. The process did not end with the telling. It had only begun.

I heard story after story. Once a member of the WELL slipped into   12
a coma in the Far East, was taken home to California through other members' efforts, then tried to recount what being in a coma was like. Another member agonized on line whether to have an elderly diabetic relative's leg amputated, detailing her dilemma and her decision. Families recount tragedies and struggles; multiple-sclerosis victims connect with one another; people look for work, find friends.

I realized quickly that technological ignorance matters little. The   13
cyber-towns are not about technology. They are about something much more basic and timeless. People get excited about one another's tales and ideas, not about the means by which they are transmitted. Stories are the heart of it, underlying all the numbing techno-talk. As I wrestled with strange commands, many of which did not work or were not entered properly, with messages that got lost or with prompts that took me places I didn't want to go and couldn't get out of, a friend asked why I was going through it all. For the stories. I wanted to hear theirs; I wanted to tell mine.

The stories are told, not written. They lack the structure and form of   14
journalist stories, and the sometimes self-conscious tone of the novel. Since most of the creators are not consciously creating art, their work is generally simple and unadorned. The tellers are preoccupied with the stories themselves, not the manner in which they are presented.

I'm outside of Cleveland, heading for I-80, and I see this bubble in my mirror, and it's a Smokey. "Radar clocked you doing 85," he says, reaching for his ticket book. I'm about to squawk when we hear this horn and this Chevy comes barreling off the road. This man jumps out, screaming that his wife is having a baby, and he says he thinks the baby is choking on the cord. The cop and I are in the car in a flash, pulling the mother out. She's in mid-delivery, and the husband is about to pass out. So the cop turns to me and says, "You up for this?" and I said I was a paramedic in Vietnam, so we lie a blanket down, slide the baby out, unwrap the cord from the baby's neck. It was beautiful and weird. Ambulance comes, husband is very grateful, so is the wife, the cop and I shake hands like we're identical twins, we recap, each of us telling the other what a hero we are and slap each other on the back. I say, "Hey, I'm overdue on this run," and he says, "Good trip, but wait a minute." He finishes writing the ticket. Can you believe cops?

—From Sandy and Eddie's Truckers
computer bulletin board

All of a sudden, this morning I realized that I was old. That's just it. I never noticed it before, not really. I realized that there was no longer any given week in which I didn't have a doctor's appointment. I can't help but notice my diminishing energy. It is more difficult to hear, to see, to endure long walks, the cold, the heat. I have a more difficult time walking my black lab on a leash. I see from my friends that a broken limb is not a small matter. We are not back on our feet in a matter of weeks. Often it is the beginning of a fearful and eternal process—operations, recovery in bed, which weakens our limbs, our muscles, makes us more brittle, nursing or hospital care that clouds our minds, confuses us. My children are angry with me. They want me to be vital, helpful, present, and they simply can't accept that I can't.

—From the computer bulletin board
Prodigy

For decades, it was television that tantalized us with the promise of 15 bringing the world into our homes. But it was difficult and expensive to get to stories, to transmit film and to broadcast them. And we rarely got to tell our own. Television was controlled by a handful of companies. So were Hollywood, book publishing and the other distributors of our culture.

By the 80's, cable, VCR's, videocams, satellites, public-access chan- 16 nels and computers began to give ordinary people the chance to tell their own stories via a variety of media. Few of these new creators would define themselves as artists; few critics would define such work as art. But anyone with a home entertainment system and a cable hookup became, in effect, an independent production company, wresting control from network programmers. Anyone with a camcorder became a journalist. On Camnet, the amateur video network shown two days a month in hundreds of thousands of American homes, anyone with a camcorder and a story can tell it and distribute it nationwide. The idea that we could share and shape our own stories in these new media began to grow.

All the talk of fiber optics and broadbands, the obsession with the   17
machinery that transmits stories, might make these forms of media seem complex, but the stories themselves are not at all arcane. They are, in fact, familiar, echoing themes and notions that date back to the recorded birth of produced storytelling.

"In drama," writes Daniel Boorstin in *The Creators,* "man found   18
ways to create unique events for delight, reflection, and dismay, and so make experience outlast the actor. The role of spectator, the person who stood outside the action, was not obvious, for the shared communal experience was overwhelming." In ancient Greece, he continues, "we see the slow stages by which man discovered that he need not always be a participant. In a new kind of immortality man could now outlive his time, relive earlier times, foreshadow later times by witnessing actors on a stage."

Mr. Boorstin could as well have been writing about cyber-space as   19
the birth of the spectator in the seventh century B.C. Amid the clacking of keyboards creating and distributing stories on line, storytellers share the communal experiences of life, death, work, love, family.

> Do you have any idea what it is like to be gay? To have to hide the most important thing about yourself, even though you had no choice about it? To live in terror of discovery? To be laughed at, isolated and beaten up. To live around people who hide their children from you? Who wouldn't let you teach them if they knew? Because I am a teacher who dreads every call to the principal's office. I always wonder if it will be my last. How can you love a country that finds you too disgusting to serve? That permits people to attack you and your friends, throw things at them from car windows, deny them the right to be married, have families? Can you conceive of that? Does this get through to you on any level at all?
>
> Two years ago, my lover and I walked through the French Quarter of New Orleans. We vacationed there because we knew it to be a tolerant place. We left a restaurant just off Bourbon Street, and three men jumped out of their cars. They knocked my lover and me down. They kicked us in the face, in the kidneys, in the groin. They knocked four of my teeth out, broke my jaw. Then they urinated on us. They laughed and said they were soldiers. That they'd love to have us in the military. I couldn't tell the police what happened. I was afraid the school district might find out back home.
>
> —From the computer bulletin board
> Compuserve

And a reply:

> I was very touched by your message, buddy. What happened to you was horrible, unsupportable. That's not what I lost three toes for in Vietnam,

for scum to beat up on people like you and your friend. I fought so you could do whatever you wanted so long as you didn't hurt anybody or break the law. You and I have no quarrel. But we do have these problems, and I'll be straight with you about it, just like you were with me. Do you have any idea what it's like to be in a field or jungle or valley with bullets and shells blowing up all around you? With your friends being cut down, ripped apart, bleeding, dying right next to you screaming for their moms or kids or wives? Do you know how much trust and communication it takes to get through that? Do you have any idea what it's like to go through that if there's tension among you?

I'm not saying this can't be worked out. I'm saying, go slow. Don't come in here with executive orders and try to change things in a day that should take longer. Don't make me into a bigot because I know it takes an unbelievable amount of feeling to crawl down there into a valley of death. It takes love of your buddy. And that's something both of us can understand, right? But if you hate him, or fear him or don't understand him—how can you do it?

It is individuals, the cyber-artists—writers and poets—who benefit   20
the most dramatically from sharing their work in so revolutionary a way. In the cyber-world, there are no agents to send back your manuscript, no editors to tell you your ideas aren't really what they have in mind, no producers to say your play can't draw an audience. Everyone's stories have an equal shot, if not equal weight. Everyone has an audience. In cyber-space, poets always have audiences.

It is not a perfect world. There are cyber-addicts who never seem to   21
get off-line. The pompous and combative can still run amok. The techno-wizards are impossible to keep up with, speaking their own language in their own world. Many people find that no amount of cyber-communication is as satisfying, meaningful or enduring as personal contact. But the stories pouring over phone lines all over the world all day long can haunt you.

I don't feel clear much any more. Good luck to everybody. It was really great talking to all of you. I loved hearing about your lives and your work and your kids. I would have loved to have had some, but not in this world. Maybe the next. I loved hearing about your screwed-up personal lives. In comparison, I felt almost normal for the first time in my life, which is weird, considering I was dying. I felt like I had the best, most loving family in the world. Sorry when I got angry, but I couldn't stay angry here for long. Looking forward to a peaceful transition for me, and for all of you. For my sake, I hope there is a God, even though D says if there was, he/she wouldn't have killed me this way.

—From the electronic diary of a
computer bulletin board member
who died of AIDS

QUESTIONS FOR DISCUSSION

1   According to Jon Katz, how has storytelling become more "democratic" in the era of the Internet and computer bulletin boards? Do you agree?

2   Katz includes a number of stories and testimonies posted on-line. Why does he arrange them as he does? How do they help illustrate his points?

3   The on-line community the WELL is described in the essay as a sort of improvisational troupe—a writer's theater where each member is at the same time "audience, performer, and scriptwriter." Do you think this sort of community can be helpful for writers, or might it be just a way of killing time, an outlet for gossip and procrastination?

4   How do the WELL members help each other out during hard times? What aspects of traditional society might this kind of electronic interaction help replace?

5   How does Katz's use of comments on ancient drama from Boorstin's *The Creators* shed light on the role of the spectator-participant in cyberspace? Is this reference relevant and insightfully applied?

IDEAS FOR WRITING

1   Follow a thread of conversation from an on-line discussion group on a serious topic such as AIDS or racism. Write an essay in which you define the typical level of development and expression you encountered. How do the postings you found compare with those in Katz's essay, and what conclusions might you draw from your findings?

2   Write an essay in which you respond to Katz's view of how on-line postings are influencing the way people write, publish, and read. What kind of influence do you think that Internet-based communications will have on how people read and write over the next few years?

Subliminal Images

BYRON REEVES AND CLIFFORD NASS

Byron Reeves and Clifford Nass are professors of communication at Stanford University who head the research group Social Responses to Communication Technologies, a project at Stanford's Institute for Communication Research of the Department of Communication and the Center for the Study of Language and Information. From their studies of human interaction with computers and other information technologies, they have concluded that people tend to perceive and relate to media-generated "personalities" such as the "voice" of a "talking" computer as if they were relating to actual human beings. Out of this research have come numerous conference presentations and publications in journals and anthologies focusing on communications and media research. In 1996 Reeves and Nass published their findings in The Media Equation: How People Treat Computers, Television and New Media Like Real People and Places. *The following selection from* The Media Equation *examines the impact on consumers of "subliminal" messages not perceivable directly to the conscious mind.*

It's important that the first few minutes of a research presentation   1
go well. In our own presentations, we usually have an introduction that is well planned and well rehearsed. During this introduction, we make eye contact with people in the audience, but we're mostly occupied with what to say next. If asked to report about how the audience was responding, we'd have a difficult time reporting accurately about whether there were smiles or frowns.

Or would we? Psychologists have accumulated a lot of evidence to   2
suggest that we had indeed processed the faces in the audience, but unconsciously. While we couldn't report *in words* what the faces looked like, if forced to guess how the talk was going, we would be able to describe, with better-than-chance accuracy, whether the presentation was a boom or a bust.

Psychologists call this research area "semantic activation without   3
subjective awareness." This means that people can think about things without knowing why. There are several kinds of experiments in this area, but the same basic idea cuts across them all: Things that we're not aware of can influence how we think and what we think about.

One type of experiment in this area uses the *dichotic listening* task.   4
Dichotic listening occurs when a person hears two conversations at once. This is sometimes referred to as the "cocktail party" task, because it simulates what many people do when several conversations are going on at once—they converse with a partner but eavesdrop on everyone else.

Psychologists have studied dichotic listening by asking people to   5
listen to conversations through stereophonic headphones. The voice
of the main speaker is presented in only one ear. People are then
asked to speak aloud (or "shadow") the speech coming to that ear.
While people shadow the main speaker, a separate voice is routed to
the other ear. Shadowing requires a great deal of focus, and because
of this, people *report* not being able to understand anything that the
second speaker says.

Subjective experience, however, is often wrong. Even though people   6
don't *think* that they hear anything that the second speaker says, when
they are asked to make guesses, they are correct at a rate better than
chance. Something gets through, though not consciously.

Another experimental task used to study unconscious processing   7
looks at the effects of quickly flashed words that appear next to, and
usually slightly before, other words. People are asked to concentrate
on the center of a display. They are told that a word will appear there,
and when it does, they will have to identify it as quickly as possible.
Just before the display is shown, a different word is flashed in another
area of the display. Since viewers are asked to focus on the center, the
other word is seen only in parafoveal vision.

Visual acuity is not good in parafoveal vision, and quickly flashed   8
information there usually cannot be identified. Nonetheless, evidence shows that information in parafoveal vision has an effect. If the
word in peripheral vision is "boat," for example, people can more
quickly identify the word "water" than unrelated words.

Unconscious Processing of Media

Our question was whether unconscious processing works any dif-   9
ferently when it unfolds in media. The possibility that media influence
the unconscious has certainly been a popular one, and the addition of
computing to the media mix has only heightened interest in what has
come to be known as subliminal persuasion. Given the computer's
ability to manipulate content quickly, might it be even better at subliminal seduction?

The literature about subliminal persuasion already includes some   10
of the most popular books about media this century. The possibility
that dastardly media folks are hiding pictures in magazine ads or
quickly flashing commercial messages in movies is captivating. When
reading about this topic, you'll find claims that pictures of genitalia
are hidden among ice cubes in magazine liquor ads, and you'll read
about pictures of popcorn boxes inserted into feature films to bolster
sales at intermission. The books discuss fantastic theories but they
lack good evidence to bolster the claims. We tried to remedy this
problem with an experiment that tested whether or not people would

use media information without being consciously aware that it had influenced their judgments.

From the psychology literature that showed how this process works in the real world, we made the following prediction about how it might work with television: 11

> Rule 1: Images in television messages that people cannot consciously identify will influence how people make judgments about media.

Creating Subliminal Content

For this experiment, we used one other technique from the psychology literature. It is called "backward pattern masking." Psychologists quickly flash images and then measure the influence of the images on how people evaluate material presented after the images appear. In these experiments, researchers first determine how long a picture must be shown for people to be able to identify it. Once this threshold is known, they then test what happens when the picture is presented for *less* time than it takes to consciously identify. 12

In these experiments, an image is first presented too fast to be consciously seen. Then, a different picture is presented, and participants are asked to identify the second picture as quickly as possible. The result? Even pictures that people cannot see can affect how quickly they identify the second picture. 13

We wanted to see whether evidence of unconscious processing could be found using the pattern masking technique with standard television equipment and typical television content. Does evidence from psychology, based on rules about how perception works, generalize to media? 14

Inserting Subliminal Messages in Traditional Media

For the experiment, we chose television segments that showed people talking in news shows, advertisements, and dramatic programs. After participants watched each one, we asked them to evaluate the emotional state of the person on the screen: Was the person happy or sad? 15

Before viewers made the evaluations, we quickly flashed one of two pictures on the screen. One was a happy face, the other a sad one. The quickly flashed pictures were our best approximation of backward pattern masking—but on television. 16

The sequence for each segment began with an orange circle shown in the middle of the screen accompanied by a voice that said, "Please look at the orange dot now." We did this because we wanted 17 to ensure that attention was directed at the screen and not elsewhere in the room.

The next image was the subliminal part. We quickly flashed either the happy or the sad face. The idea was that the emotion of the face would influence the evaluation of the video segment that followed. After the picture of the smiling or frowning face was shown, we showed a patterned mask, which is a black-and-white picture of geometric shapes. Without the mask, the image of the face would linger on the retina, and viewers would have more time to identify and consider the initial face. 18

The critical feature of the flashed pictures was their duration. Each of the two faces was shown for either one video frame or two video frames, and there is something very important about the difference. If you show a smiling face for one video frame (33 milliseconds), and then follow it immediately with one frame of a patterned mask, it is *impossible* for people to tell what was in the picture. Everyone is aware that *something* happened (it looks like a flashbulb went off), but no one can tell that they saw a picture of a face. 19

If the picture of the face is on the screen for two video frames, however, no one has a problem identifying the contents of the picture. This difference represents the two levels of awareness used in the psychology experiments. One frame equals no subjective awareness; two frames equals definite subjective awareness. 20

After the face and patterned mask, we showed a longer television segment. Viewers held a joystick that they used to evaluate the person in each segment. Pushing the stick to the right meant that they thought the person in the segment was happy; pushing to the left meant the person in the segment was sad. 21

Effectiveness of Subliminal Messages

One result was that when viewers could clearly identify the happy face, they thought that the people in the segments that followed were themselves happier. And the opposite was true for the sad face. In other words, *priming* works. What you see at one moment activates a way of thinking that influences subsequent evaluations. People just can't switch gears that quickly. 22

Strikingly, the same priming effect occurred when viewers had no conscious knowledge about the picture that was flashed at them. When the flash was a happy face, the people that followed seemed more happy. When the flash was a sad face, the people that followed seemed more sad. Quickly flashed pictures that conveyed emotion became active in viewers' minds, even though the viewers had no subjective awareness of their presence. 23

What Subliminal Effects Are—and Aren't

What we don't see or notice can have an effect in media just as in   24
real life. The media delivering the information need not be compli-
cated: The effect works with a standard VCR and television set. This
result is one more indication that media are not special with regard to
how information is processed psychologically.

It is important to note, however, that the results are not like most of   25
the popular notions about subliminal persuasion. Subliminal effects
in the popular literature are mostly about ambiguous forms or at least
ones that are hard to see; for example, body parts or words hidden
in pictures. This study, and the other psychological research as well,
used pictures and words that were explicit and obvious. We doubt that
the experiment would have worked if the pictures were fuzzy or otherwise disguised.

The popular notions of subliminal persuasion also assume a   26
process of unconscious influence that is considerably more complex.
The popular argument is that subliminal experience is generalized to
something that is apparently *un*related to the initial information. For
example, the letters S E and X, rendered imprecisely in ice cubes, are
said to generalize to a product in the same picture. The argument is
that the letters will bring to mind the word "sex," which will then make
people think about sexual images, which will then make people feel
good and aroused, which will then influence what they think of a particular brand of vodka poured over the cubes. This is a complex series
of generalizations, much more complex than is demonstrated in our
study, and a sequence that we think is unlikely.

Subliminal Content in New Media

The specific design implications of this discussion are pretty simple,   27
and different for television as compared to newer media. For broadcast television, subliminal persuasion, at least in the form of quickly
flashed pictures and words, is banned by the Federal Communication
Commission. This has been true since the 1970s, when controversy
erupted over a TV ad for a memory game called Husker Du that dis-
played the words, "Get it," on the screen for a fraction of a second.

Computers and software, however, are *un*regulated. There are no   28
official prohibitions of these techniques anywhere in the world of
multimedia. Consequently, the issue of subliminal persuasion has
gained new life. Designers and the public now discuss subliminal
effect in *multi*media—everything from advertisements embedded in
screen savers to attempts to bolster employee morale with hidden
messages flashed on networked computers. One of the more interesting aspects of these discussions is that it might be easier to accomplish

subliminal intrusions with a computer than with a television, because software can respond to the particular input of individual users and timing is more precise. Of course, ethical and legal issues abound.

QUESTIONS FOR DISCUSSION

1   What do the phenomena of "dichotic listening" and "parafoveal vision" reveal about the possibility of effective subliminal persuasion in the media?

2   To what degree do Reeves and Nass believe that our processing of media information is unconscious? Do you agree with their position?

3   What experiment did the authors design in order to test their prediction that unconsciously perceived television images can influence people's judgment? Does the experiment seem valid?

4   How were the results of the authors' experiment different from the popular views of "subliminal persuasion"?

5   What is the legal difference between the use of subliminal persuasion in television and its use in computer-based multimedia? What are the implications of the difference in regulation? How is computer software particularly useful for those interested in developing subliminal persuasion?

IDEAS FOR WRITING

1   There has been considerable discussion of the need to regulate the conscious, overt content of violent video games and the Internet, but little or no discussion of the subliminal or covert content of such media. Write an essay in which you argue for or against the need for and practicality of regulation of the possible subliminal appeals of the new electronic media.

2   Do some research into the effectiveness of subliminal persuasion in television or other electronic media, and write a cause-and-effect essay based on your findings.

Don't Look Back

STEVEN HOLTZMAN

Steven Holtzman's interests lie in the areas of computers, philosophy, and creativity. He holds an undergraduate degree in Western and Eastern philosophy and a Ph.D. in computer science from the University of Edinburgh, and he is founder and vice president of Optimal Networks in Palo Alto, California. Using computer techniques, he has composed a number of musical works that have been performed in Europe and the United States. Holtzman has written two books that examine the new types of creative expression possible in the age of computers and cyberspace: Digital Mantras: The Language of Abstract and Virtual Worlds *(1995) and* Digital Mosaics: The Aesthetics of Cyberspace *(1997). The books are aesthetically appealing as well as intellectually provocative. In the following excerpt from* Digital Mosaics, *he argues that we can't turn our backs on digital technology, for it is already inextricably a part of our lives.*

For centuries, the book has been the primary vehicle for recording, storing, and transferring knowledge. But it's hard to imagine that paper will be the preferred format in a hundred years. Digital media will marginalize this earlier form of communication, relegating it to a niche just as music CDs have replaced LPs. The book will be forced to redefine itself, just as TV forced radio to redefine itself, and radio and TV together transformed the newspaper's role. The process is survival of the fittest—competition in the market to be a useful medium. Whatever the book's future is, clearly its role will never be the same. The book has lost its preeminence.   1

The print medium of newspaper is also fading. Almost every major newspaper in the United States is experiencing significant declines in circulation. (The exception is *USA Today*—characterized by itself as "TV on paper.") More than 70 percent of Americans under the age of thirty don't read newspapers. And this trend isn't about to change.   2

The powers of the media business today understand this. As part of the frenzied convergence of media, communications, and the digital world, we're witnessing a dizzying tangle of corporate alliances and mega-mergers. Companies are jockeying for position for this epochal change. The list includes many multibillion-dollar companies—AT&T, Bertelsmann, Disney, Microsoft, Time Warner, Viacom—and many, many more small startup technology companies. They all want to position themselves as preeminent new media companies.   3

Clinging to the Past

Members of the literary establishment can also see this imminent change. Yet, for the most part, they take a dim view of these new digital   4 worlds. Beyond the loss of their cherished culture, what disturbs many critics is that they find new digital media like CD-ROMs and the World Wide Web completely unsatisfying.

The literary critic Sven Birkerts eloquently laments that the generation growing up in the digital age is incapable of enjoying literature. Teaching at college has brought Birkerts to despair because his students aren't able to appreciate the literary culture he so values. After only a proudly self-confessed "glimpse of the future" of CD-ROMs, he declares he is "clinging all the more tightly to my books."   5

· The disillusionment with the digital experience is summed up by the *New York Times Book Review* critic Sarah Lyall. She complains that multimedia CD-ROMs   6

> still don't come close to matching the experience of reading a paper-and-print book while curled up in a chair, in bed, on the train, under a tree, in an airplane. . . . After all, the modern book is the result of centuries of trial and error during which people wrote on bark, on parchment, on vellum, on clay, on scrolls, on stone, chiseling characters into surfaces or copying them out by hand.

Okay, I thought as I read Birkerts and Lyall, these are members of a dying cultural heritage who—like seemingly every generation—are uncomfortable with the new. Unable to shift their perspective, they'll be casualties of change. After all, Birkerts boasts that he doesn't own a computer and still uses only a typewriter.   7

Birkerts clings not to his books, but to the past. I was reminded of a comment by the cultural critic William Irwin Thompson, who is also wary of the consequences of digital technology: 8

> It is not the literary intelligentsia of *The New York Review of Books* [or *The New York Times*, as the case may be] that is bringing forth this new culture, for it is as repugnant to them as the Reformation was to the Catholic Church. . . . This new cyberpunk, technological culture is brought forth by Top and Pop, electronic science and pop music, and both the hackers and the rockers are anti-intellectual and unsympathetic to the previous Mental level expressed by the genius of European civilization.

This helped me dismiss the backlash from those looking in the rearview mirror. But then I came across a book by Clifford Stoll.

Muddier Mud

Stoll, who was introduced to computers twenty years ago, is a long-time member of the digerati. In his book *Silicone Snake Oil*, he claims to expose the true emptiness of the digital experience.   9

In opening, Stoll explains that "every time someone mentions MUDs [multi-user dungeons, a type of interactive adventure game] and virtual reality, I think of a genuine reality with muddier mud than anything a computer can deliver." Stoll then nostalgically recounts   10 the story of the first time he went crawling through caves in his college days. "We start in, trailing a string through the muddy tunnel—everything's covered with gunk, as are the six of us crawling behind [the guide]. Not your ordinary slimy, brown, backyard mud, either. This is the goop of inner-earth that works its way into your hair, socks, and underwear."

Stoll's general theme: "You're viewing a world that doesn't exist. 11 During that week you spend on-line, you could have planted a tomato garden. . . . While the Internet beckons brightly, seductively flashing an icon of knowledge-as-power, this nonplace lures us to surrender our time on earth."

I suppose this excludes any experience that might distract us from 12 the real—a novel, a Beethoven symphony, a movie. (A tomato garden?)

And then we get the same theme that Birkerts and Lyall hit on. 13

> I've rarely met anyone who prefers to read digital books. I don't want my morning newspaper delivered over computer, or a CD-ROM stuffed with National Geographic photographs. Call me a troglodyte; I'd rather peruse those photos alongside my sweetheart, catch the newspaper on the way to work, and page through a real book. . . . Now, I'm hardly a judge of aesthetics, but of the scores of electronic multimedia productions I've seen, I don't remember any as being beautiful.

A CD-ROM Is Not a Book

These laments totally miss the point. No, a CD-ROM isn't a book. 14 Nor is a virtual world—whether a MUD or a simulation of rolling in the mud—the same as the real experience. This is *exactly* the point! A CD-ROM isn't a book; it's something completely new and different. A MUD on the Internet isn't like mud in a cave. A virtual world isn't the real world; it offers possibilities unlike anything we've known before.

Birkerts, Lyall, and Stoll dismiss the digital experience to justify 15 staying in the familiar and comfortable worlds of their past. Yet what's exciting to me about these digital worlds is precisely that they're new, they're unfamiliar, and they're our future.

It's not that I disagree with the literati's assertions. We will lose part 16 of our literary culture and tradition. Kids today are so attuned to the rapid rhythms of MTV that they're unresponsive to the patient patterns of literary prose. They are indeed so seduced by the flickeringly powerful identifications of the screen as to be deaf to the inner voices of print. Literary culture—like classical music and opera—will become marginalized as mainstream culture pursues a digital path.

There never will be a substitute for a book. And today's multimedia 17 CD-ROM—even surfing the World Wide Web—is still for the most part a static and unsatisfying experience. But it's rather early to conclude anything about their ultimate potential.

Patience Is a Virtue

It puzzles me that there are people who expect that, in almost no   18
time at all, we'd find great works by those who have mastered the
subtleties of such completely new digital worlds. We are seeing the
first experiments with a new medium. It took a long time to master
the medium of film. Or the book, for that matter. It will also take time
to master new digital worlds.

It's challenging to create a multimedia digital world today. The   19
enabling technologies that will make radically new digital worlds
possible—Java, VRML, and a string of acronymic technologies—are
still emerging. Artists, writers, and musicians must also be software
programmers. Today, a rare combination of passion, artistry, and
technical knowledge is required. Yet, over time, these skills will become common. Even more important than the technical mastery of
new digital media, a new conceptual framework and aesthetic must
also be established for digital worlds.

When this conceptual and technical mastery is achieved, we'll dis-   20
cover the true possibilities of digital expression. In a few decades—or
possibly in just five years—we'll look on today's explorations as primitive. Until then, we will continue to explore these new digital worlds
and seek to learn their true potential.

Embracing the Digital

There will be nothing to replace the reading of a book or newspaper   21
in bed. Curling up by a fireside to read a poem with an electronic tablet
won't have the same intimacy as doing so with a book. But curling up
by a fireside with an electronic tablet is itself simply an example of sub-
stituting electronic technology for an existing medium—extrapolating
from today's flat-paneled handheld computers to an "electronic book."
We need to develop a new aesthetic—a digital aesthetic. And the
emerging backlash from the literati makes clear to me how urgently
we need it.

When we've mastered digital media, we won't be talking about any-   22
thing that has much to do with the antiquated form of the book. I
imagine myself curled up in bed with laser images projected on my
retinas, allowing me to view and travel through an imaginary three-
dimensional virtual world. A story about the distant past flashes a
quaint image of a young woman sitting and reading a book, which
seems just as remote as the idea of a cluster of Navajo Indians sitting
around a campfire and listening to a master of the long-lost tradition
of storytelling. In a hundred years, we'll think of the book as we do the
storyteller today.

Will we lose a part of our cultural heritage as we assimilate new   23
media? No doubt. Is this disturbing? Absolutely. Today's traditional

media will be further marginalized. Is there much value in decrying an inevitable future? Probably not. The music of *today* is written on electric instruments. Hollywood creates our theater. And soon digital media will be *our* media. Digital technology and new digital media—for better or worse—are here to stay.

That's not to say that all things digital are good. Perhaps, like the   24 Luddites in Britain during the first half of the nineteenth century, the literati raise a flag of warning, raise awareness, and create debate, debunking some of the myths of a utopian digital future. But in the end, for better or for worse, the efforts of the Luddites were futile when it came to stopping the industrial revolution.

Likewise, today you can't turn off the Internet. Digital technology   25 isn't going away. There are already thousands of multimedia CD-ROMs and hundreds of thousands of sites on the World Wide Web; soon there will be thousands of channels of on-demand digital worlds.

Digital technology is part of our lives, a part of our lives that we   26 know will only continue to grow. We can't afford to dismiss it. Rather we must embrace it—not indiscriminately, but thoughtfully. We must seize the opportunities generated by the birth of a new medium to do things we've never been able to do before. Don't look back.

QUESTIONS FOR DISCUSSION

1   Why does Holtzman believe the power and popularity of books and newspapers are fading? Do you agree?

2   According to William Thompson, why do the members of the "literary intelligentsia" find the new culture of CD-ROMs and the Internet so repugnant? What other reasons for the rejection might there be?

3   What is computer scientist Cliff Stoll's primary reason for rejecting the Internet as a learning experience for children? How does Holtzman attempt to refute Stoll? Is he successful?

4   What features of the book appear to the traditional critics as irreplaceable? Does the argument of these critics seem valid?

5   What do you think Holtzman means by his concluding statement that we must embrace digital media "not indiscriminately, but thoughtfully"? Do you think his essay is a good example of the thoughtful approach he recommends? Why or why not?

IDEAS FOR WRITING

1   Write an essay in which you compare your own experience with the World Wide Web or a learning program on a multimedia CD-ROM disk to reading a regular book or textbook on the same

subject. Explain which experience you found more useful and worthwhile, and why.

2   Write a comparison of your experience of learning from the physical world through direct experience as opposed to learning about the same subject through using a multimedia CD-ROM or the Internet. Do you agree with Cliff Stoll that direct experience is the preferable way to learn? Why or why not?

CONNECTIONS: TOPICS FOR THOUGHT, RESEARCH, AND WRITING

1   Taking into consideration the influence of musical figures discussed in the essays by Crouch, hooks, and Brubach, pick out several key figures in popular music from the past few decades and discuss how each embodies the spirit and values of his or her times. For a stronger focus, you might limit yourself to musicians of a particular gender or ethnic background.

2   Write an essay in which you give examples and respond to the commercialization of some of the icons of pop culture such as Madonna, Mickey Mouse, or Michael Jackson through spinoffs such as clothes, toys, and games. Do you think that this commercialization process weakens or strengthens the power of the original icon?

3   Considering portrayals of the American family in the media as presented by Winn, Gates, and others, write an essay in which you argue whether the fictional media families of today have much basis in reality or influence on actual American family life.

4   New communications media often have been seen as ushering in a period of broadened perceptions, new prosperity, and vast educational benefits. Taking into consideration works such as those of Brautigan, Katz, Kantrowitz, and Holtzman, argue whether such assumptions and claims currently being made for computers and the Internet have validity.

5   Some media and social critics have viewed the rise of new communication technologies as a threat to traditional standards of morality and social order. Taking into account essays by such writers as Winn, Bok, Males, Holtzman, and hooks, pick a particular communications medium you are interested in. Write an essay in which you provide examples of the fears of destructive social influence that surround it. Do these fears seem justified?

6   Media critics such as Gates, hooks, Kantrowitz, and Williams have commented on the lack of presence of or distorted images of women and minority groups in electronic media and cyberspace. Pick a group that you feel is particularly underrepresented or unfairly stereotyped in the media, and make some suggestions for increasing the positive exposure for this group.

7   Media critics have referred to computers and cyberspace as an "electronic frontier," because the new electronic media have evolved so fast that there are no viable standards of control or censorship over content and access. Taking into account the ideas of Kantrowitz, Katz, Williams, Holtzman, and Reeves and Nass, do you believe that further legal regulation is necessary for the Internet, and if so, what kind?

8   Considering the ideas of critics such as Scholes, Katz, Reeves and Nass, and Holtzman, contrast the way you would read a particular book or other print-based information source with the way you would come to understand a multimedia source on a similar subject, such as a video adaptation of a novel or a multimedia encyclopedia entry.

9   Write an essay analyzing one or two of the following films, considering issues raised in this book about the relationship between society and technological change in the electronic communications media: *Alphaville* (1965), *Nashville* (1975), *Network* (1976), *Quiz Show* (1993), *Bladerunner* (1982/1992), *Cinema Paradiso* (1990), *Harrison Bergeron* (1995), *The Net* (1995), *Johnny Mnemonic* (1995), or *Boogie Nights* (1997).

Acknowledgments

Sissela Bok, "Aggression: The Impact of Media Violence," from *Mayhem: Violence as Public Entertainment,* pages 82–89. Copyright © 1998 by Sissela Bok. Reprinted by permission of Addison Wesley Longman.

Richard Brautigan, "All Watched Over by Machines of Loving Grace," from *The Pill Versus the Springhill Mine Disaster.* Copyright © 1969 by Richard Brautigan. Reprinted by permission of Houghton Mifflin Company. All rights reserved.

Holly Brubach, "The Age of the Female Icon," from *New York Times Magazine,* November 24, 1996. Copyright © 1996 by The New York Times. Reprinted by permission.

Stanley Crouch, "The King of Narcissism," from *Always in Pursuit,* Pantheon, 1998. Copyright © 1998 by Stanley Crouch. Reprinted by permission of the author.

Henry Louis Gates, Jr., "The Living Room," from *Colored People.* Copyright © 1994 by Henry Louis Gates, Jr. Reprinted by permission of Alfred A. Knopf, Inc.

Steven Holtzman, "Don't Look Back," reprinted with the permission of Simon & Schuster from *Digital Mosaics: The Aesthetics of Cyberspace.* Copyright © 1997 by Steven Holtzman.

bell hooks, "Gangsta Culture—Sexism, Misogyny: Who Will Take the Rap?" from *Outlaw Culture: Resisting Representations.* Copyright © 1994 by Gloria Watkins. Reproduced by permission of Routledge, Inc.

Barbara Kantrowitz, "Men, Women, and Computers," from *Newsweek,* May 16, 1994. Copyright © 1994 by Newsweek, Inc. All rights reserved. Reprinted by permission.

Jon Katz, "The Tales They Tell in Cyber-Space Are a Whole Other Story," from the *New York Times,* January 23, 1994. Reprinted by permission of Sterling Lord Literistic, Inc. Copyright © 1994 by Jon Katz.

Mike Males, "Who Us? Stop Blaming Kids and TV," from *The Progressive,* October 1997. Reprinted by permission of *The Progressive,* 409 E. Main Street, Madison, WI 53703.

Byron Reeves and Clifford Nass, "Subliminal Images," from *The Media Equation: How People Treat Computers, Television, and New Media Like Real People and Places.* Copyright © 1996 by Cambridge University Press. Reprinted with the permission of Cambridge University Press.

Robert Scholes, "On Reading a Video Text," from *Protocols of Reading.* Copyright © 1989 by Yale University Press. Reprinted by permission of Yale University Press.

Acknowledgments (continued)

Patricia J. Williams, "Hate Radio," from *Ms.,* Vol. 4, No. 5 (March–April 1994): 25. Reprinted by permission of Ms. Magazine, © 1994.

Marie Winn, "Family Life," from *The Plug-in Drug,* rev. ed. Copyright © 1977, 1985 by Marie Winn Miller. Used by permission of Viking Penguin, a division of Penguin Putnam, Inc.

John Updike, "The Mystery of Mickey Mouse," from *Arts and Antiques,* November 1991. Reprinted by permission of the author.